Winnie-the-Pooh

Pu der Bär

[Bilingual Edition]

English – German

by A. A. Milne

Translated by Möwenstein

ISBN: 979-8-89513-054-4

Original text: *Winnie-the-Pooh* (1926) by A. A. Milne (1882-1956)

This bilingual edition—including translation, editorial revisions, formatting, and supplementary content—is produced and edited by Mowenstein Books LLC, with the original text faithfully reproduced from public-domain sources.

While every effort has been made to ensure accuracy, minor discrepancies may occur. Readers are encouraged to consult the original text for reference.

Cover Art: Inspired by *Hustling Sunlight* by Matthew Bakkom (www.hustlingsunlight.xyz)

Möwenstein Books™ is a trademark of and imprint published by Mowenstein Books LLC.

For permissions or inquiries:

Website: mowenstein.com
Email: copyright@mowenstein.com

Mowenstein Books LLC
DE, USA

Contents

WINNIE-THE-POOH

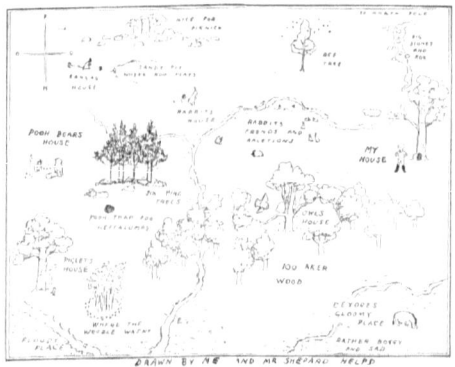

CHAPTER I

KAPITEL I

2.1 Here is Edward Bear, coming downstairs now, bump, bump, bump, on the back of his head, behind Christopher Robin.

Hier ist Edward Bär, der jetzt die Treppe herunterkommt, bump, bump, bump, auf dem Hinterkopf, hinter Christopher Robin.

It is, as far as he knows, the only way of coming downstairs, but sometimes he feels that there really is another way, if only he could stop bumping for a moment and think of it. 2.2

Das ist, soweit er weiß, die einzige Möglichkeit, die Treppe hinunter zu kommen, aber manchmal hat er das Gefühl, dass es wirklich einen anderen Weg gibt, wenn er nur für einen Moment aufhören könnte zu stoßen und daran denken könnte.

And then he feels that perhaps there isn't. 2.3

Und dann hat er das Gefühl, dass es vielleicht gar keinen gibt.

Anyhow, here he is at the bottom, and ready to be introduced to you. 2.4

Wie auch immer, hier ist er unten und bereit, Ihnen vorgestellt zu werden.

Winnie-the-Pooh. 2.5

Winnie-the-Pooh.

When I first heard his name, I said, just as you are going to say, 3.1

Als ich seinen Namen zum ersten Mal hörte, sagte ich, so wie Sie jetzt sagen werden,

"But I thought he was a boy?" 3.2

"Aber ich dachte, er sei ein Junge?"

"So did I," said Christopher Robin. 4.1

"Ich auch," sagte Christopher Robin.

"Then you can't call him Winnie?" 5.1

"Dann kannst du ihn nicht Winnie nennen?"

6.1 "I don't."
"Ich nicht."

7.1 "But you said —— "
"Aber Sie sagten —— "

8.1 "He's Winnie-ther-Pooh. Don't you know what 'ther'
"Er ist Winnie-ther-Pooh. Weißt du nicht, was 'ther'

8.2 means?"
bedeutet?"

9.1 "Ah, yes, now I do," I said quickly;
"Ah, ja, jetzt weiß ich es," sagte ich schnell;

9.2 and I hope you do too, because it is all the explanation you are going to get.
und ich hoffe, Sie wissen es auch, denn das ist die einzige Erklärung, die Sie bekommen werden.

10.1 Sometimes Winnie-the-Pooh likes a game of some sort when he comes downstairs, and sometimes he likes to sit quietly in front of the fire and listen to a story.
Manchmal mag Winnie-the-Pooh eine Art Spiel, wenn er nach unten kommt, und manchmal sitzt er gerne still vor dem Kamin und hört einer Geschichte zu.

10.2 This evening ——
Heute Abend ——

11.1 "What about a story?" said Christopher Robin.
"Wie wäre es mit einer Geschichte?" fragte Christopher Robin.

"What about a story?" I said.   12.1
"Wie wäre es mit einer Geschichte?" sagte ich.

"Could you very sweetly tell Winnie-the-Pooh one?"   13.1
"Könntest du Winnie-the-Pooh eins sagen?"

"I suppose I could," I said.   14.1
"Das könnte ich wohl," sagte ich.

"What sort of stories does he like?"   14.2
"Was für Geschichten mag er denn?"

"About himself. Because he's that sort of Bear."   15.1
"Über sich selbst. Weil er diese Art von Bär ist."

"Oh, I see."   16.1
"Oh, ich verstehe."

"So could you very sweetly?"   17.1
"Könntest du also ganz lieb sein?"

"I'll try," I said.   18.1
"Ich werde es versuchen," sagte ich.

So I tried.   19.1
Also habe ich es versucht.

21.1 Once upon a time, a very long time ago now, about last Friday, Winnie-the-Pooh lived in a forest all by himself under the name of Sanders.

Es war einmal, vor sehr langer Zeit, ungefähr am vergangenen Freitag, da lebte Winnie-the-Pooh ganz allein in einem Wald und hieß Sanders.

23.1 ("What does 'under the name' mean?"

("Was bedeutet 'unter dem Namen'?"

23.2 asked Christopher Robin.

fragte Christopher Robin.

24.1 "It means he had the name over the door in gold letters,

"Es bedeutet,

24.2 and lived under it."

dass er den Namen in goldenen Lettern über der Tür hatte und darunter wohnte."

"Winnie-the-Pooh wasn't quite sure," 25.1
"Winnie-the-Pooh war sich nicht ganz sicher,"

said Christopher Robin. 25.2
sagte Christopher Robin.

"Now I am," said a growly voice. 26.1
"Jetzt bin ich es," sagte eine knurrige Stimme.

"Then I will go on," said I.) 27.1
"Dann werde ich weitergehen," sagte ich.)

One day when he was out walking, he came to an 28.1
open place in the middle of the forest, and in the
middle of this place was a large oak-tree, and, from
the top of the tree, there came a loud buzzing-noise.
Als er eines Tages spazieren ging, kam er an einen offenen
Platz mitten im Wald, und in der Mitte dieses Platzes stand
eine große Eiche, und aus der Spitze des Baumes kam ein
lautes Brummen.

Winnie-the-Pooh sat down at the foot of the tree, 30.1
Winnie-the-Pooh setzte sich an den Fuß des Baumes,

30.2 **put his head between his paws and began to think.**
steckte den Kopf zwischen die Pfoten und begann zu
überlegen.

31.1 **First of all he said to himself:**
Zuerst sagte er zu sich selbst:

31.2 **"That buzzing-noise means something.**
"Dieses Brummen bedeutet etwas.

31.3 **You don't get a buzzing-noise like that, just buzzing
and buzzing, without its meaning something.**
Es gibt kein solches Summen, das nur summt und brummt,
ohne dass es etwas bedeutet.

31.4 **If there's a buzzing-noise, somebody's making a
buzzing-noise, and the only reason for making a
buzzing-noise that I know of is because you're a bee."**
Wenn es brummt, macht jemand ein Brummgeräusch, und
der einzige Grund für ein Brummgeräusch, den ich kenne,
ist, dass du eine Biene bist."

32.1 **Then he thought another long time, and said:**
Dann dachte er wieder lange nach und sagte:

32.2 **"And the only reason for being a bee that I know of is
making honey."**
"Und der einzige Grund, eine Biene zu sein, den ich kenne,
ist, Honig zu machen."

33.1 **And then he got up, and said:**
Und dann stand er auf und sagte:

"And the only reason for making honey is so as I can eat it."

33.2

"Und der einzige Grund, warum ich Honig mache, ist, dass ich ihn essen kann."

So he began to climb the tree.

33.3

So begann er auf den Baum zu klettern.

He climbed and he climbed and he climbed, and as he climbed he sang a little song to himself.

35.1

Er kletterte und kletterte und kletterte, und während er kletterte, sang er sich ein kleines Lied vor.

It went like this:

35.2

Es ging so:

Isn't it funny

36.1

Ist es nicht lustig

37.1 **How a bear likes honey?**
Wie mag ein Bär Honig?

38.1 **Buzz! Buzz! Buzz!**
Buzz! Buzz! Buzz!

39.1 **I wonder why he does?**
Ich frage mich, warum er das tut?

40.1 **Then he climbed a little further ...**
Dann kletterte er noch ein bisschen weiter ...

40.2 **and a little further ...**
und noch ein bisschen weiter ...

40.3 **and then just a little further.**
und dann nur noch ein bisschen weiter.

40.4 **By that time he had thought of another song.**
Inzwischen hatte er sich ein anderes Lied ausgedacht.

41.1 **It's a very funny thought that, if Bears were Bees,**
Es ist ein sehr lustiger Gedanke, dass, wenn Bären Bienen wären,

42.1 **They'd build their nests at the**
Sie bauten ihre Nester an der

43.1 **bottom**
unten

44.1 **of trees.**
von Bäumen.

And that being so (if the Bees were Bears), 45.1
Und wenn das so wäre (wenn die Bienen Bären wären),

We shouldn't have to climb up all these stairs. 46.1
Wir sollten nicht all diese Treppen hinaufsteigen müssen.

He was getting rather tired by this time, 47.1
Er war inzwischen ziemlich müde geworden,

so that is why he sang a Complaining Song. 47.2
deshalb sang er ein Klagelied.

He was nearly there now, 47.3
Er war jetzt fast da,

and if he just stood on that branch ... 47.4
und wenn er nur auf dem Ast stehen würde ...

Crack! 48.1
Crack!

"Oh, help!" said Pooh, 49.1
"Oh, Hilfe!" sagte Pooh,

as he dropped ten feet on the branch below him. 49.2
als er zehn Fuß tief auf den Ast unter ihm fiel.

51.1 "If only I hadn't —— " he said,
"Hätte ich nur nicht ...," sagte er,

51.2 as he bounced twenty feet on to the next branch.
als er zwanzig Fuß auf den nächsten Ast sprang.

52.1 "You see, what I meant to do,"
"Siehst du, was ich vorhatte,"

52.2 he explained, as he turned head-over-heels, and
crashed on to another branch thirty feet below,
erklärte er, als er sich kopfüber auf einen anderen Ast
stürzte, der dreißig Fuß tiefer lag,

52.3 "what I meant to do —— "
"was ich vorhatte ..."

53.1 "Of course, it was rather —— " he admitted,
"Natürlich war es ziemlich ..." gab er zu,

as he slithered very quickly through the next six branches.

während er sehr schnell durch die nächsten sechs Äste schlitterte.

53.2

"It all comes, I suppose,"

"Das kommt wohl alles davon,"

54.1

he decided, as he said good-bye to the last branch, spun round three times, and flew gracefully into a gorse-bush,

beschloss er, als er sich vom letzten Zweig verabschiedete, sich dreimal drehte und anmutig in einen Ginsterstrauch flog,

54.2

"it all comes of liking honey so much. Oh, help!"

"das kommt davon, dass ich den Honig so sehr mag. Oh, Hilfe!"

54.3

He crawled out of the gorse-bush, brushed the prickles from his nose, and began to think again.

Er kroch aus dem Ginsterbusch, bürstete sich die Stacheln aus der Nase und begann wieder zu denken.

55.1

And the first person he thought of was Christopher Robin.

Und die erste Person, an die er dachte, war Christopher Robin.

55.2

57.1 ("Was that me?"
("War ich das?"

57.2 said Christopher Robin in an awed voice, hardly daring to believe it.
sagte Christopher Robin mit ehrfürchtiger Stimme und wagte es kaum zu glauben.

58.1 "That was you."
"Das warst du."

59.1 Christopher Robin said nothing, but his eyes got larger and larger, and his face got pinker and pinker.)
Christopher Robin sagte nichts, aber seine Augen wurden immer größer und sein Gesicht wurde immer rosiger.)

60.1 So Winnie-the-Pooh went round to his friend Christopher Robin,
Also ging Winnie-the-Pooh zu seinem Freund Christopher Robin,

60.2 who lived behind a green door in another part of the forest.
der hinter einer grünen Tür in einem anderen Teil des Waldes wohnte.

"Good morning, Christopher Robin," he said. 62.1
"Guten Morgen, Christopher Robin," sagte er.

"Good morning, Winnie-ther-Pooh," said you. 63.1
"Guten Morgen, Winnie-ther-Pooh," sagst du.

"I wonder if you've got such a thing as a balloon 64.1
about you?"
"Ich frage mich, ob du so etwas wie einen Ballon in dir
trägst?"

"A balloon?" 65.1
"Ein Luftballon?"

"Yes, I just said to myself coming along: 66.1
"Ja, ich habe gerade zu mir selbst gesagt:

'I wonder if Christopher Robin has such a thing as a 66.2
balloon about him?'
'Ich frage mich, ob Christopher Robin so etwas wie einen
Luftballon an sich hat?'

66.3 I just said it to myself, thinking of balloons, and wondering."

Ich sagte es einfach zu mir selbst, dachte an Luftballons und fragte mich."

67.1 "What do you want a balloon for?" you said.

"Wozu brauchst du einen Luftballon?" hast du gefragt.

68.1 Winnie-the-Pooh looked round to see that nobody was listening, put his paw to his mouth, and said in a deep whisper:

Winnie-the-Pooh schaute sich um, um zu sehen, dass niemand zuhörte, legte seine Pfote an den Mund und sagte mit einem tiefen Flüsterton:

68.2 "Honey!"

"Schatz!"

69.1 "But you don't get honey with balloons!"

"Aber mit Luftballons bekommt man keinen Honig!"

70.1 "I do," said Pooh.

"Ich schon," sagte Pooh.

71.1 Well, it just happened that you had been to a party the day before at the house of your friend Piglet, and you had balloons at the party.

Nun, es war so, dass du am Tag zuvor bei deinem Freund Ferkel auf einer Party warst, und du hattest Luftballons auf der Party.

You had had a big green balloon; and one of Rabbit's relations had had a big blue one, and had left it behind, being really too young to go to a party at all; and so you had brought the green one and the blue one home with you. 71.2

Du hattest einen großen grünen Ballon, und ein Verwandter von Kaninchen hatte einen großen blauen, den er zurückgelassen hatte, weil er noch zu jung war, um überhaupt auf eine Party zu gehen.

"Which one would you like?" you asked Pooh. 72.1

"Welches möchtest du haben?" fragst du Pooh.

He put his head between his paws and thought very carefully. 73.1

Er steckte den Kopf zwischen die Pfoten und dachte sehr sorgfältig nach.

"It's like this," he said. 74.1

"Es ist so," sagte er.

"When you go after honey with a balloon, the great thing is not to let the bees know you're coming. 74.2

"Wenn man mit einem Ballon auf Honigsuche geht, ist es wichtig, dass die Bienen nicht wissen, dass man kommt.

Now, if you have a green balloon, they might think you were only part of the tree, and not notice you, and, if you have a blue balloon, they might think you were only part of the sky, and not notice you, and the question is: 74.3

Wenn du einen grünen Ballon hast, könnten sie denken, du wärst nur ein Teil des Baumes und dich nicht bemerken, und wenn du einen blauen Ballon hast, könnten sie denken, du wärst nur ein Teil des Himmels und dich nicht bemerken, und die Frage ist:

74.4 Which is most likely?"

Was ist am wahrscheinlichsten?"

75.1 "Wouldn't they notice you underneath the balloon?" you asked.

"Würden sie dich unter dem Ballon nicht bemerken?" fragst du.

76.1 "They might or they might not," said Winnie-the-Pooh.

"Vielleicht, vielleicht auch nicht," sagte Winnie-the-Pooh.

76.2 "You never can tell with bees."

"Bei Bienen kann man das nie wissen."

76.3 He thought for a moment and said:

Er dachte einen Moment nach und sagte dann:

76.4 "I shall try to look like a small black cloud.

"Ich werde versuchen, wie eine kleine schwarze Wolke auszusehen.

76.5 That will deceive them."

Das wird sie täuschen."

19

"Then you had better have the blue balloon," 78.1

"Dann nimmst du besser den blauen Ballon,"

you said; and so it was decided. 78.2

sagtest du, und so wurde es beschlossen.

Well, you both went out with the blue balloon, and 80.1
you took your gun with you, just in case, as you
always did, and Winnie-the-Pooh went to a very
muddy place that he knew of, and rolled and rolled
until he was black all over;

Nun, ihr seid beide mit dem blauen Ballon losgezogen, und
du hast dein Gewehr mitgenommen, nur für den Fall, wie
du es immer tust, und Winnie-the-Pooh ist zu einer sehr
schlammigen Stelle gegangen, die er kannte, und hat sich
gerollt und gerollt, bis er ganz schwarz war;

and then, when the balloon was blown up as big as 80.2
big, and you and Pooh were both holding on to the
string, you let go suddenly, and Pooh Bear floated
gracefully up into the sky, and stayed there — level
with the top of the tree and about twenty feet away
from it.

und dann, als der Ballon so groß wie groß aufgeblasen war
und du und Pooh euch beide an der Schnur festhielten,
habt ihr plötzlich losgelassen, und Pooh Bear schwebte
anmutig in den Himmel hinauf und blieb dort, auf der
Höhe der Baumkrone und etwa zwanzig Fuß von ihr
entfernt.

82.1 "Hooray!" you shouted.
"Hurra!" riefst du.

83.1 "Isn't that fine?"
"Ist das nicht schön?"

83.2 shouted Winnie-the-Pooh down to you.
rief Winnie-the-Pooh zu dir herunter.

83.3 "What do I look like?"
"Wie sehe ich denn aus?"

84.1 "You look like a Bear holding on to a balloon,"
"Du siehst aus wie ein Bär, der sich an einem Luftballon festhält,"

84.2 you said.
hast du gesagt.

85.1 "Not," said Pooh anxiously,
"Nicht," sagte Puuh ängstlich,

85.2 " — not like a small black cloud in a blue sky?"
"nicht wie eine kleine schwarze Wolke am blauen Himmel?"

86.1 "Not very much."
"Nicht sehr viel."

"Ah, well, perhaps from up here it looks different. 87.1

"Na ja, von hier oben sieht es vielleicht anders aus.

And, as I say, you never can tell with bees." 87.2

Und wie gesagt, bei Bienen kann man nie wissen."

There was no wind to blow him nearer to the tree, so 88.1
there he stayed.

Es gab keinen Wind, der ihn näher zum Baum geblasen
hätte, also blieb er dort.

He could see the honey, he could smell the honey, but 88.2
he couldn't quite reach the honey.

Er konnte den Honig sehen, er konnte den Honig riechen,
aber er konnte ihn nicht erreichen.

After a little while he called down to you. 89.1

Nach einer Weile rief er zu Ihnen herunter.

"Christopher Robin!" he said in a loud whisper. 90.1

"Christopher Robin!" flüsterte er laut.

"Hallo!" 91.1

"Hallo!"

"I think the bees suspect something!" 92.1

"Ich glaube, die Bienen ahnen etwas!"

"What sort of thing?" 93.1

"Was für eine Sache?"

"I don't know. 94.1

"Ich weiß es nicht.

94.2 But something tells me that they're suspicious!"

Aber etwas sagt mir, dass sie verdächtig sind!"

96.1 "Perhaps they think that you're after their honey."

"Vielleicht denken sie, dass du hinter ihrem Honig her bist."

97.1 "It may be that. You never can tell with bees."

"Das kann sein. Bei Bienen kann man das nie wissen."

98.1 There was another little silence,

Es herrschte wieder ein kurzes Schweigen,

98.2 and then he called down to you again.

und dann rief er wieder zu Ihnen herunter.

99.1 "Christopher Robin!"

"Christopher Robin!"

100.1 "Yes?"

"Ja?"

"Have you an umbrella in your house?"   101.1
"Haben Sie einen Regenschirm im Haus?"

"I think so."   102.1
"Ich glaube schon."

"I wish you would bring it out here, and walk up   103.1
and down with it, and look up at me every now and
then, and say
"Ich wünschte, du würdest sie hierher bringen, mit ihr auf
und ab gehen und ab und zu zu mir hochschauen und sagen

'Tut-tut, it looks like rain.'   103.2
'Tut-tut, es sieht nach Regen aus.'

I think, if you did that, it would help the deception   103.3
which we are practising on these bees."
Ich glaube, wenn du das tun würdest, würde es der
Täuschung helfen, die wir an den Bienen praktizieren."

Well, you laughed to yourself, "Silly old Bear."   104.1
Du hast gelacht, "Der dumme alte Bär."

but you didn't say it aloud because you were so fond   104.2
of him, and you went home for your umbrella.
aber du hast es nicht laut gesagt, weil du ihn so gern hattest,
und bist nach Hause gegangen, um deinen Regenschirm zu
holen.

106.1 "Oh, there you are!" called down Winnie-the-Pooh,
"Oh, da bist du ja!" rief Winnie-the-Pooh,

106.2 as soon as you got back to the tree.
als du zum Baum zurückkamst.

106.3 "I was beginning to get anxious.
"Ich habe schon angefangen, mir Sorgen zu machen.

106.4 I have discovered that the bees are now definitely Suspicious."
Ich habe entdeckt, dass die Bienen jetzt wirklich verdächtig sind."

107.1 "Shall I put my umbrella up?" you said.
"Soll ich meinen Schirm aufspannen?" fragten Sie.

108.1 "Yes, but wait a moment. We must be practical.
"Ja, aber warten Sie einen Moment. Wir müssen praktisch sein.

108.2 The important bee to deceive is the Queen Bee.
Die wichtigste zu täuschende Biene ist die Bienenkönigin.

Can you see which is the Queen Bee from down there?"

Kannst du von da unten sehen, welche die Bienenkönigin ist?"

"No."

"Nein."

"A pity.

"Wie schade.

Well, now, if you walk up and down with your umbrella, saying,

Nun, wenn du mit deinem Regenschirm auf und ab gehst und sagst,

'Tut-tut, it looks like rain,'

'Tut-tut, es sieht nach Regen aus,'

I shall do what I can by singing a little Cloud Song, such as a cloud might sing ...Go!"

werde ich tun, was ich kann, indem ich ein kleines Wolkenlied singe, wie es eine Wolke singen könnte ...Go!"

So, while you walked up and down and wondered if it would rain, Winnie-the-Pooh sang this song:

Während du also auf und ab gingst und dich fragtest, ob es regnen würde, sang Winnie-the-Pooh dieses Lied:

How sweet to be a Cloud

Wie süß, eine Wolke zu sein

Floating in the Blue!

Schweben im Blau!

114.1 **Every little cloud**
Jedes Wölkchen

115.1 **Always**
Immer

116.1 **sings aloud.**
singt laut.

117.1 **"How sweet to be a Cloud**
"Wie süß, eine Wolke zu sein

118.1 **Floating in the Blue!"**
Schweben im Blau!"

119.1 **It makes him very proud**
Das macht ihn sehr stolz

120.1 **To be a little cloud.**
Eine kleine Wolke zu sein.

121.1 **The bees were still buzzing as suspiciously as ever.**
Die Bienen brummten immer noch so misstrauisch wie immer.

121.2 **Some of them, indeed, left their nests and flew all round the cloud as it began the second verse of this song, and one bee sat down on the nose of the cloud for a moment, and then got up again.**
Einige von ihnen verließen sogar ihr Nest und flogen um die Wolke herum, als sie die zweite Strophe dieses Liedes anstimmte, und eine Biene setzte sich für einen Moment auf die Nase der Wolke und stand dann wieder auf.

"Christopher — ow! — Robin," called out the cloud. 123.1
"Christopher — ow! — Robin," rief die Wolke.

"Yes?" 124.1
"Ja?"

"I have just been thinking, and I have come to a very 125.1
important decision.
"Ich habe gerade nachgedacht und bin zu einer sehr
wichtigen Entscheidung gekommen.

These are the wrong sort of bees." 125.2
Das sind die falschen Bienen."

"Are they?" 126.1
"Sind sie das?"

"Quite the wrong sort. 127.1
"Ganz die falsche Sorte.

So I should think they would make the wrong sort of 127.2
honey, shouldn't you?"
Also würde ich denken, dass sie die falsche Sorte Honig
machen, oder?"

129.1 **"Would they?"**
"Würden sie?"

130.1 **"Yes. So I think I shall come down."**
"Ja. Ich denke, ich werde runterkommen."

131.1 **"How?" asked you.**
"Wie?" fragten Sie.

132.1 **Winnie-the-Pooh hadn't thought about this.**
Daran hatte Winnie-the-Pooh nicht gedacht.

132.2 **If he let go of the string,**
Wenn er die Schnur loslassen würde,

132.3 **he would fall — bump — and he didn't like the idea of that.**
würde er fallen - und das gefiel ihm nicht.

132.4 **So he thought for a long time, and then he said:**
Also dachte er lange nach, und dann sagte er:

133.1 **"Christopher Robin,**
"Christopher Robin,

you must shoot the balloon with your gun.   133.2
du musst den Ballon mit deinem Gewehr abschießen.

Have you got your gun?"   133.3
Hast du dein Gewehr dabei?"

"Of course I have," you said.   134.1
"Natürlich habe ich das," hast du gesagt.

"But if I do that, it will spoil the balloon," you said.   134.2
"Aber wenn ich das tue, ist der Ballon kaputt," sagtest du.

"But if you don't," said Pooh,   135.1
"Aber wenn du das nicht tust," sagte Pooh,

"I shall have to let go, and that would spoil me."   135.2
"muss ich loslassen, und das würde mich verderben."

When he put it like this, you saw how it was, and you   136.1
aimed very carefully at the balloon, and fired.
Als er es so formulierte, sah man, wie es war, und man
zielte sehr genau auf den Ballon und schoss.

"Ow!" said Pooh.   137.1
"Au!" sagte Puuh.

"Did I miss?" you asked.   138.1
"Habe ich etwas verpasst?" fragten Sie.

"You didn't exactly miss," said Pooh,   139.1
"Du hast ihn nicht ganz verfehlt," sagte Pooh,

"but you missed the balloon."   139.2
"aber du hast den Ballon verfehlt."

140.1 "I'm so sorry,"
"Es tut mir so leid,"

140.2 you said, and you fired again, and this time you hit the balloon, and the air came slowly out, and Winnie-the-Pooh floated down to the ground.
sagtest du, und du schießt noch einmal, und diesmal triffst du den Ballon, und die Luft entweicht langsam, und Winnie-the-Pooh schwebt zu Boden.

141.1 But his arms were so stiff from holding on to the string of the balloon all that time that they stayed up straight in the air for more than a week, and whenever a fly came and settled on his nose he had to blow it off.
Aber seine Arme waren so steif, weil er sich die ganze Zeit an der Schnur des Ballons festhielt, dass sie mehr als eine Woche lang gerade in der Luft blieben, und jedes Mal, wenn sich eine Fliege auf seiner Nase niederließ, musste er sie wegpusten.

141.2 And I think - but I am not sure -
Und ich glaube - aber ich bin mir nicht sicher -

141.3 that that is why he was always called Pooh.
dass er deshalb immer Pooh genannt wurde.

"Is that the end of the story?" asked Christopher Robin.

"Ist das das Ende der Geschichte?" fragte Christopher Robin.

143.1

"That's the end of that one. There are others."

"Das ist das Ende von diesem. Es gibt noch andere."

144.1

"About Pooh and Me?"

"Über Pooh und mich?"

145.1

"And Piglet and Rabbit and all of you. Don't you remember?"

"Und Ferkel und Hase und ihr alle. Wisst ihr nicht mehr?"

146.1

"I do remember, and then when I try to remember, I forget."

"Ich erinnere mich, und wenn ich dann versuche, mich zu erinnern, vergesse ich es wieder."

147.1

"That day when Pooh and Piglet tried to catch the Heffalump —— "

"An dem Tag, als Puuh und Ferkel versuchten, den Heffalump zu fangen ..."

148.1

"They didn't catch it, did they?"

"Sie haben ihn nicht erwischt, oder?"

149.1

"No."

"Nein."

150.1

"Pooh couldn't, because he hasn't any brain.

"Pooh könnte das nicht, weil er kein Gehirn hat.

151.1

151.2 Did I catch it?"

Habe ich es verstanden?"

152.1 "Well, that comes into the story."

"Nun, das kommt in der Geschichte vor."

153.1 Christopher Robin nodded.

Christopher Robin nickte.

154.1 "I do remember," he said,

"Ich erinnere mich," sagte er,

154.2 "only Pooh doesn't very well, so that's why he likes having it told to him again.

"nur Pooh nicht so gut, und deshalb mag er es, wenn man es ihm noch einmal erzählt.

154.3 Because then it's a real story and not just a remembering."

Denn dann ist es eine echte Geschichte und nicht nur eine Erinnerung."

155.1 "That's just how I feel," I said.

"Genau so fühle ich mich," sagte ich.

156.1 Christopher Robin gave a deep sigh, picked his Bear up by the leg, and walked off to the door, trailing Pooh behind him.

Christopher Robin stieß einen tiefen Seufzer aus, nahm seinen Bären am Bein und ging zur Tür, wobei er Puuh hinter sich her zog.

156.2 At the door he turned and said,

An der Tür drehte er sich um und sagte,

"Coming to see me have my bath?" 156.3
"Kommst du, um zu sehen, wie ich mein Bad nehme?"

"I might," I said. 157.1
"Vielleicht," sagte ich.

"I didn't hurt him when I shot him, did I?" 158.1
"Ich habe ihn doch nicht verletzt, als ich ihn erschossen habe, oder?"

"Not a bit." 159.1
"Kein bisschen."

He nodded and went out, and in a moment I heard Winnie-the- Pooh - 160.1
Er nickte und ging hinaus, und im nächsten Moment hörte ich, wie Winnie-the- Pooh -

bump, bump, bump - going up the stairs behind him. 160.2
bump, bump, bump - hinter ihm die Treppe hinaufging.

CHAPTER II · IN WHICH POOH GOES VISITING AND GETS INTO A TIGHT PLACE

KAPITEL II · IN DEM PUUH ZU BESUCH
KOMMT UND IN EINE ENGE STELLE
GERÄT

2.1 Edward Bear, known to his friends as Winnie-the-Pooh, or Pooh for short, was walking through the forest one day, humming proudly to himself.

Edward Bär, der seinen Freunden als Winnie-the-Pooh oder kurz Pooh bekannt ist, ging eines Tages durch den Wald und summte stolz vor sich hin.

He had made up a little hum that very morning, 2.2

Das Summen hatte er sich an jenem Morgen ausgedacht,

as he was doing his Stoutness Exercises in front of the glass: 2.3

als er vor dem Glas seine Steifheitsübungen machte:

Tra-la-la, tra-la-la, as he stretched up as high as he could go, and then Tra-la-la, tra-la — oh, help! 2.4

Tra-la-la, tra-la-la, als er sich so hoch streckte, wie er konnte, und dann Tra-la-la, tra-la-oh, Hilfe!

— la, as he tried to reach his toes. 2.5

— la, als er versuchte, seine Zehen zu erreichen.

After breakfast he had said it over and over to himself until he had learnt it off by heart, and now he was humming it right through, properly. 2.6

Nach dem Frühstück hatte er es sich immer wieder vorgesagt, bis er es auswendig gelernt hatte, und nun summte er es regelrecht vor sich hin.

It went like this: 2.7

Es ging ungefähr so:

Tra-la-la, tra-la-la, 3.1

Tra-la-la, tra-la-la,

Tra-la-la, tra-la-la, 4.1

Tra-la-la, tra-la-la,

Rum-tum-tiddle-um-tum. 5.1

Rum-tum-tiddle-um-tum.

6.1 **Tiddle-iddle, tiddle-iddle,**
Tiddle-iddle, tiddle-iddle,

7.1 **Tiddle-iddle, tiddle-iddle,**
Tiddle-iddle, tiddle-iddle,

8.1 **Rum-tum-tum-tiddle-um.**
Rum-tum-tum-tiddle-um.

10.1 **Well, he was humming this hum to himself, and
walking along gaily, wondering what everybody else
was doing, and what it felt like, being somebody else,
when suddenly he came to a sandy bank, and in the
bank was a large hole.**
Er summte dieses Lied vor sich hin, ging fröhlich weiter
und fragte sich, was alle anderen taten und wie es sich
anfühlte, jemand anderes zu sein, als er plötzlich an eine
sandige Bank kam, in der ein großes Loch war.

"Aha!" said Pooh. (Rum-tum-tiddle-um- tum.) 11.1
"Aha!" sagte Puuh. (Rum-tum-tiddle-um- tum.)

"If I know anything about anything, that hole means 11.2
Rabbit,"
"Wenn ich irgendetwas über irgendetwas weiß, dann
bedeutet dieses Loch Kaninchen,"

he said, "and Rabbit means Company," he said, 11.3
sagte er, "und Kaninchen bedeutet Gesellschaft," sagte er,

"and Company means Food and Listening-to-Me- 11.4
Humming and such like.
"und Gesellschaft bedeutet Essen und Hören-auf-mich-
summen und dergleichen.

Rum-tum-tum-tiddle- um." 11.5
Rum-tum-tum-tiddle- um."

So he bent down, put his head into the hole, and 12.1
called out:
Also bückte er sich, steckte seinen Kopf in das Loch und
rief:

"Is anybody at home?" 13.1
"Ist jemand zu Hause?"

There was a sudden scuffling noise from inside the 14.1
hole,
Plötzlich ertönte ein Geräusch aus dem Inneren des Lochs,

and then silence. 14.2
und dann war es still.

"What I said was, 'Is anybody at home?"' 15.1
"Ich sagte, 'Ist jemand zu Hause?"'

15.2 called out Pooh very loudly.
rief Puuh sehr laut.

16.1 "No!" said a voice; and then added,
"Nein!" sagte eine Stimme und fügte hinzu,

16.2 "You needn't shout so loud.
"Du brauchst nicht so laut zu schreien.

16.3 I heard you quite well the first time."
Ich habe dich schon beim ersten Mal sehr gut gehört."

17.1 "Bother!" said Pooh. "Isn't there anybody here at
all?"
"Ach was!" sagte Puuh. "Ist denn überhaupt niemand
hier?"

18.1 "Nobody."
"Niemand."

19.1 Winnie-the-Pooh took his head out of the hole, and
thought for a little, and he thought to himself,
Winnie-the-Pooh nahm seinen Kopf aus dem Loch und
dachte eine Weile nach, und er dachte sich,

19.2 "There must be somebody there, because somebody
must have said,
"Da muss jemand sein, denn jemand muss, gesagt haben,

19.3 'Nobody. "'
'Niemand. "'

19.4 So he put his head back in the hole, and said:
Also steckte er seinen Kopf wieder in das Loch und sagte:

"Hallo, Rabbit, isn't that you?"
20.1
"Hallo, Hase, bist du das nicht?"

"No," said Rabbit,
21.1
"Nein," sagte Kaninchen,

in a different sort of voice this time.
21.2
diesmal mit einer anderen Art von Stimme.

"But isn't that Rabbit's voice?"
22.1
"Aber ist das nicht die Stimme von Rabbit?"

"I don't think so," said Rabbit.
23.1
"Das glaube ich nicht," sagte Kaninchen.

"It isn't meant to be."
23.2
"Es soll nicht sein."

"Oh!" said Pooh.
24.1
"Oh!" sagte Puuh.

He took his head out of the hole, and had another
25.1
think, and then he put it back, and said:
Er nahm seinen Kopf aus dem Loch, dachte noch einmal
nach, steckte ihn wieder hinein und sagte, "Ich will nicht,
dass du mich verrätst:

"Well, could you very kindly tell me where Rabbit is?"
26.1
"Könnten Sie mir freundlicherweise sagen, wo Rabbit ist?"

"He has gone to see his friend Pooh Bear,
27.1
"Er ist zu seinem Freund Puuh-Bär gegangen,

27.2 **who is a great friend of his."**
der ein guter Freund von ihm ist."

28.1 **"But this is Me!" said Bear, very much surprised.**
"Aber das bin doch ich!" sagte Bär sehr überrascht.

29.1 **"What sort of Me?"**
"Was für ein Ich?"

30.1 **"Pooh Bear."**
"Puuh- Bär."

31.1 **"Are you sure?" said Rabbit, still more surprised.**
"Bist du dir sicher?" fragte Kaninchen noch erstaunter.

32.1 **"Quite, quite sure," said Pooh.**
"Ganz, ganz sicher," sagte Puuh.

33.1 **"Oh, well, then, come in."**
"Na gut, dann komm rein."

So Pooh pushed and pushed and pushed his way
through the hole,
35.1

Also schob und schob und schob Puuh seinen Weg durch
das Loch,

and at last he got in.
35.2

und schließlich kam er hinein.

"You were quite right,"
36.1

"Du hattest recht,"

said Rabbit, looking at him all over.
36.2

sagte Rabbit und sah ihn von oben bis unten an.

"It is you. Glad to see you."
36.3

"Du bist es. Ich freue mich, dich zu sehen."

"Who did you think it was?"
37.1

"Was dachtest du, wer es ist?"

"Well, I wasn't sure.
38.1

"Nun, ich war mir nicht sicher.

You know how it is in the Forest.
38.2

Du weißt ja, wie es im Wald ist.

One can't have anybody coming into one's house.
38.3

Man kann niemanden in sein Haus lassen.

One has to be careful.
38.4

Man muss vorsichtig sein.

What about a mouthful of something?"
38.5

Wie wäre es mit einem Schluck von irgendetwas?"

39.1 Pooh always liked a little something at eleven o'clock
in the morning, and he was very glad to see Rabbit
getting out the plates and mugs;

Puuh mochte immer eine Kleinigkeit um elf Uhr morgens,
und er war sehr froh, als Rabbit die Teller und Tassen
herausholte;

39.2 and when Rabbit said,

und als Rabbit sagte,

39.3 "Honey or condensed milk with your bread?"

"Honig oder Kondensmilch zu deinem Brot?"

39.4 he was so excited that he said, "Both,"

war er so aufgeregt, dass er sagte, "Beides,"

39.5 and then, so as not to seem greedy, he added,

und dann, um nicht gierig zu wirken, fügte er hinzu,

39.6 "But don't bother about the bread, please."

"Aber mach dir bitte keine Sorgen um das Brot."

39.7 And for a long time after that he said nothing ...

Und danach sagte er lange Zeit nichts mehr ...

39.8 until at last, humming to himself in a rather sticky
voice, he got up, shook Rabbit lovingly by the paw,
and said that he must be going on.

bis er schließlich, vor sich hin summend und mit ziemlich
klebriger Stimme, aufstand, Kaninchen liebevoll an der
Pfote schüttelte und sagte, dass er weitergehen müsse.

40.1 "Must you?" said Rabbit politely.

"Musst du das?" sagte Kaninchen höflich.

"Well," said Pooh, 41.1

"Nun," sagte Pooh,

"I could stay a little longer if it — if you —— " 41.2

"ich könnte noch ein bisschen bleiben, wenn ...,"

and he tried very hard to look in the direction of the 41.3
larder.

und er bemühte sich sehr, in Richtung Speisekammer zu
schauen.

"As a matter of fact," said Rabbit, 42.1

"In der Tat," sagte Rabbit,

"I was going out myself directly." 42.2

"ich wollte gerade selbst hinausgehen."

"Oh, well, then, I'll be going on. Good- bye." 43.1

"Nun gut, dann gehe ich jetzt weiter. Auf Wiedersehen."

"Well, good-bye, if you're sure you won't have any 44.1
more."

"Nun, auf Wiedersehen, wenn Sie sicher sind, dass Sie
nicht noch mehr haben wollen."

"Is there any more?" asked Pooh quickly. 45.1

"Gibt es noch mehr?" fragte Pooh schnell.

Rabbit took the covers off the dishes, and said, "No, 46.1

Kaninchen nahm die Abdeckungen vom Geschirr und
sagte, "Nein,

there wasn't." 46.2

da war nichts."

47.1 "I thought not," said Pooh, nodding to himself. "Well,

"Dachte ich mir," sagte Pooh und nickte vor sich hin. "Nun,

47.2 good-bye. I must be going on."

auf Wiedersehen. Ich muss jetzt weiter."

49.1 So he started to climb out of the hole.

Also begann er, aus dem Loch zu klettern.

49.2 He pulled with his front paws, and pushed with his back paws, and in a little while his nose was out in the open again ...and then his ears ...and then his front paws ...and then his shoulders ...and then ——

Er zog mit den Vorderpfoten und schob mit den Hinterpfoten, und nach kurzer Zeit war seine Nase wieder im Freien ...und dann seine Ohren ...und dann seine Vorderpfoten ...und dann seine Schultern ...und dann ...

50.1 "Oh, help!" said Pooh. "I'd better go back."

"Oh, Hilfe!" sagte Puuh. "Ich gehe besser zurück."

51.1 "Oh, bother!" said Pooh. "I shall have to go on."

"Oh, Mist!" sagte Puuh. "Ich muss weitermachen."

"I can't do either!" said Pooh. "Oh, help and bother!" 52.1

"Ich kann beides nicht," sagte Pooh. "Oh, Hilfe und Mühe!"

Now by this time Rabbit wanted to go for a walk too, 53.1
and finding the front door full, he went out by the
back door, and came round to Pooh, and looked at
him.

Nun wollte auch der Hase spazieren gehen, und da er die
Vordertür voll hatte, ging er durch die Hintertür hinaus,
kam zu Puuh und sah ihn an.

"Hallo, are you stuck?" he asked. 55.1

"Hallo, steckst du fest?" fragte er.

"N-no," said Pooh carelessly. 56.1

"N-nein," sagte Puuh achtlos.

"Just resting and thinking and humming to myself." 56.2

"Ich ruhe mich nur aus, denke nach und summe vor mich
hin."

"Here, give us a paw." 57.1

"Hier, gib uns eine Pfote."

58.1 Pooh Bear stretched out a paw,
Puuh-Bär streckte eine Pfote aus,

58.2 and Rabbit pulled and pulled and pulled ...
und Kaninchen zog und zog und zog ...

59.1 "Ow!" cried Pooh. "You're hurting!"
"Au!" schrie Puuh. "Du tust mir weh!"

60.1 "The fact is," said Rabbit, "you're stuck."
"Tatsache ist," sagte Rabbit, "du steckst fest."

61.1 "It all comes," said Pooh crossly,
"Das kommt alles daher," sagte Pooh verärgert,

61.2 "of not having front doors big enough."
"dass die Haustüren nicht groß genug sind."

62.1 "It all comes," said Rabbit sternly,
"Das kommt alles," sagte Kaninchen streng,

62.2 "of eating too much. I thought at the time," said
Rabbit,
"vom zu viel Essen. Ich dachte damals," sagte Kaninchen,

62.3 "only I didn't like to say anything," said Rabbit,
"ich wollte nur nichts sagen," sagte Kaninchen,

62.4 "that one of us was eating too much," said Rabbit,
"dass einer von uns zu viel gegessen hatte," sagte
Kaninchen,

62.5 "and I knew it wasn't me," he said.
"und ich wusste, dass ich es nicht war," sagte er.

"Well, well, I shall go and fetch Christopher Robin." 62.6
"Nun gut, ich werde gehen und Christopher Robin holen."

Christopher Robin lived at the other end of the Forest, 63.1
and when he came back with Rabbit, and saw the
front half of Pooh, he said,
Christopher Robin wohnte am anderen Ende des Waldes,
und als er mit Rabbit zurückkam und die vordere Hälfte
von Pooh sah, sagte er mit so liebevoller Stimme,

"Silly old Bear," 63.2
"Dummer alter Bär,"

in such a loving voice that everybody felt quite 63.3
hopeful again.
dass alle wieder Hoffnung schöpften.

"I was just beginning to think," 64.1
"Ich habe gerade angefangen zu denken,"

said Bear, sniffing slightly, 64.2
sagte Bär und schniefte leicht,

"that Rabbit might never be able to use his front door 64.3
again.
"dass Rabbit vielleicht nie wieder seine Haustür benutzen
kann.

And I should hate that," he said. 64.4
Und das würde ich hassen," sagte er.

"So should I," said Rabbit. 65.1
"Das sollte ich auch," sagte Kaninchen.

66.1 "Use his front door again?" said Christopher Robin.
"Wieder seine Haustür benutzen?" fragte Christopher
Robin.

66.2 "Of course he'll use his front door again."
"Natürlich wird er seine Haustür wieder benutzen."

67.1 "Good," said Rabbit.
"Gut," sagte Kaninchen.

68.1 "If we can't pull you out, Pooh, we might push you
back."
"Wenn wir dich nicht herausziehen können, Pooh,
schieben wir dich vielleicht zurück."

69.1 Rabbit scratched his whiskers thoughtfully, and
pointed out that, when once Pooh was pushed back,
he was back, and of course nobody was more glad to
see Pooh than he was, still there it was, some lived in
trees and some lived underground, and ——
Kaninchen kratzte sich nachdenklich an den
Schnurrhaaren und wies darauf hin, dass, wenn Pooh
einmal zurückgestoßen war, er wieder da war, und
natürlich freute sich niemand mehr als er, Pooh zu sehen,
dennoch war es so, manche lebten auf Bäumen und manche
lebten unter der Erde, und- -

70.1 "You mean I'd never get out?" said Pooh.
"Du meinst, ich komme nie wieder raus?" sagte Pooh.

71.1 "I mean," said Rabbit,
"Ich meine," sagte Rabbit,

"that having got so far, it seems a pity to waste it." 71.2
"dass es schade ist, es zu verschwenden, nachdem wir so
weit gekommen sind."

Christopher Robin nodded. 72.1
Christopher Robin nickte.

"Then there's only one thing to be done," he said. 73.1
"Dann bleibt uns nur eines übrig," sagte er.

"We shall have to wait for you to get thin again." 73.2
"Wir müssen darauf warten, dass du wieder dünn wirst."

"How long does getting thin take?" asked Pooh 74.1
anxiously.
"Wie lange dauert es, dünn zu werden?" fragte Puuh
ängstlich.

"About a week, I should think." 75.1
"Etwa eine Woche, denke ich."

"But I can't stay here for a week!" 76.1
"Aber ich kann nicht eine Woche lang hier bleiben!"

"You can stay here all right, silly old Bear. 77.1
"Du kannst ruhig hier bleiben, dummer alter Bär.

It's getting you out which is so difficult." 77.2
Es ist so schwierig, dich herauszuholen."

"We'll read to you," said Rabbit cheerfully. 78.1
"Wir werden dir vorlesen," sagte Hase fröhlich.

50

78.2 **"And I hope it won't snow," he added.**
"Und ich hoffe, es schneit nicht," fügte er hinzu.

78.3 **"And I say, old fellow, you're taking up a good deal of room in my house — do you mind if I use your back legs as a towel-horse?**
"Und ich sage dir, alter Freund, du nimmst eine Menge Platz in meinem Haus ein - macht es dir etwas aus, wenn ich deine Hinterbeine als Handtuchpferd benutze?

78.4 **Because, I mean, there they are — doing nothing — and it would be very convenient just to hang the towels on them."**
Denn ich meine, sie stehen da und tun nichts, und es wäre sehr praktisch, die Handtücher daran aufzuhängen."

79.1 **"A week!" said Pooh gloomily.**
"Eine Woche!" sagte Puuh düster.

79.2 **"What about meals?"**
"Was ist mit den Mahlzeiten?"

80.1 **"I'm afraid no meals," said Christopher Robin,**
"Ich fürchte, es gibt kein Essen," sagte Christopher Robin,

80.2 **"because of getting thin quicker. But we will read to you."**
"weil wir schneller dünn werden. Aber wir werden dir vorlesen."

Bear began to sigh, and then found he couldn't
because he was so tightly stuck; and a tear rolled
down his eye, as he said:

81.1

Der Bär begann zu seufzen und merkte dann, dass er es
nicht konnte, weil er so feststeckte, und eine Träne kullerte
über sein Auge, als er sagte:

"Then would you read a Sustaining Book,

82.1

"Würdest du dann ein unterstützendes Buch lesen,

such as would help and comfort a Wedged Bear in
Great Tightness?"

82.2

wie es einem verkeilten Bären in großer Enge helfen und
ihn trösten würde?"

So for a week Christopher Robin read that sort of
book at the North end of Pooh,

84.1

Eine Woche lang las Christopher Robin diese Art von Buch
am nördlichen Ende von Pooh,

and Rabbit hung his washing on the South end ...

84.2

und Rabbit hängte seine Wäsche am südlichen Ende auf ...

84.3 **and in between Bear felt himself getting slenderer and slenderer.**

und dazwischen fühlte sich Bär immer schlanker und schlanker.

84.4 **And at the end of the week Christopher Robin said, "Now!"**

Und am Ende der Woche sagte Christopher Robin, "Jetzt!"

86.1 **So he took hold of Pooh's front paws and Rabbit took hold of Christopher Robin, and all Rabbit's friends and relations took hold of Rabbit, and they all pulled together ...**

Also hielt er sich an Puuhs Vorderpfoten fest, und Kaninchen hielt sich an Christopher Robin fest, und alle Freunde und Verwandten von Kaninchen hielten sich an Kaninchen fest, und sie zogen alle zusammen ...

87.1 **And for a long time Pooh only said "Ow!" ...**

Und lange Zeit sagte Puuh nur "Au!" ...

88.1 **And "Oh!" ...**

Und "Oh!" ...

And then, all of a sudden, he said "Pop!"

90.1

Und dann sagte er plötzlich "Pop!"

just as if a cork were coming out of a bottle.

90.2

als würde ein Korken aus einer Flasche kommen.

And Christopher Robin and Rabbit and all Rabbit's friends and relations went head-over-heels backwards...

91.1

Und Christopher Robin und Kaninchen und alle Freunde und Verwandten von Kaninchen gingen kopfüber rückwärts...

and on the top of them came Winnie-the-Pooh — free!

91.2

und auf ihnen kam Winnie-the-Pooh frei!

So, with a nod of thanks to his friends, he went on with his walk through the forest, humming proudly to himself.

92.1

Mit einem dankenden Nicken an seine Freunde setzte er seinen Spaziergang durch den Wald fort und brummte stolz vor sich hin.

92.2 **But, Christopher Robin looked after him lovingly, and said to himself,**

Aber Christopher Robin schaute ihm liebevoll nach und sagte zu sich selbst,

92.3 **"Silly old Bear!"**

"Dummer alter Bär!"

CHAPTER III · IN WHICH POOH AND PIGLET GO HUNTING AND NEARLY CATCH A WOOZLE

KAPITEL III · IN DEM PUUH UND FERKEL AUF DIE JAGD GEHEN UND BEINAHE EINEN WOOZLE FANGEN

1.1 The Piglet lived in a very grand house in the middle of a beech-tree, and the beech-tree was in the middle of the forest, and the Piglet lived in the middle of the house.

Das Ferkel wohnte in einem sehr großen Haus in der Mitte einer Buche, und die Buche stand mitten im Wald, und das Ferkel wohnte in der Mitte des Hauses.

1.2 Next to his house was a piece of broken board which had:

Neben seinem Haus war ein Stück kaputtes Brett, auf dem stand:

1.3 "TRESPASSERS W" on it.

"TRESPASSERS W" darauf stand.

When Christopher Robin asked the Piglet what it   1.4
meant, he said it was his grandfather's name, and had
been in the family for a long time, Christopher Robin
said you couldn't be called Trespassers W, and Piglet
said yes, you could, because his grandfather was, and
it was short for Trespassers Will, which was short for
Trespassers William.

Als Christopher Robin das Ferkel fragte, was das bedeute,
sagte es, es sei der Name seines Großvaters, und schon
lange in der Familie sei; Christopher Robin sagte, man
könne nicht Trespasser W heißen, und Ferkel sagte, "Doch,
das kann man, denn sein Großvater hieß so, und das war
die Abkürzung für Trespassers Will, was wiederum die
Abkürzung für Trespassers William war.

And his grandfather had had two names in case he   1.5
lost one —

Und sein Großvater hatte zwei Namen, falls er einen
verlor —

Trespassers after an uncle, and William after   1.6
Trespassers.

Trespassers, nach einem Onkel, und William, nach
Trespassers.

3.1 "I've got two names," said Christopher Robin
carelessly.

"Ich habe zwei Namen," sagte Christopher Robin achtlos.

4.1 "Well, there you are, that proves it," said Piglet.

"Da hast du es, das beweist es," sagte Ferkel.

5.1 One fine winter's day when Piglet was brushing away
the snow in front of his house, he happened to look
up, and there was Winnie-the-Pooh.

An einem schönen Wintertag, als Ferkel den Schnee vor
seinem Haus wegfegte, schaute er zufällig auf, und da war
Winnie-the-Pooh.

5.2 Pooh was walking round and round in a circle,
thinking of something else, and when Piglet called
to him, he just went on walking.

Puuh ging im Kreis herum und dachte an etwas anderes,
und als Ferkel ihm zurief, ging er einfach weiter.

6.1 "Hallo!" said Piglet, "what are you doing?"

"Hallo!" sagte Ferkel, "was machst du da?"

7.1 "Hunting," said Pooh.

"Jagen," sagte Puuh.

8.1 "Hunting what?"

"Was jagen?"

9.1 "Tracking something,"

"Etwas aufspüren,"

9.2 said Winnie-the-Pooh very mysteriously.

sagte Winnie-the-Pooh sehr geheimnisvoll.

"Tracking what?" said Piglet, coming closer. 10.1

"Was aufspüren?" fragte Ferkel und kam näher.

"That's just what I ask myself. I ask myself, What?" 11.1

"Das ist genau das, was ich mich frage. Ich frage mich,
"Was?"

"What do you think you'll answer?" 12.1

"Was glauben Sie, was Sie antworten werden?"

"I shall have to wait until I catch up with it," 13.1

"Ich werde warten müssen, bis ich es einhole,"

said Winnie-the-Pooh. "Now, look there." 13.2

sagte Winnie-the-Pooh. "Nun, schau mal da."

He pointed to the ground in front of him. 13.3

Er zeigte auf den Boden vor ihm.

"What do you see there?" 13.4

"Was siehst du da?"

"Tracks," said Piglet. "Paw- marks." 15.1

"Spuren," sagte Ferkel. "Pfotenabdrücke."

60

15.2 He gave a little squeak of excitement. "Oh, Pooh!
Er quietschte ein wenig vor Aufregung. "Oh, Puuh!

15.3 Do you think it's a — a — a Woozle?"
Meinst du, es ist ein Woozle?"

16.1 "It may be," said Pooh. "Sometimes it is,
"Das mag sein," sagte Pooh. "Manchmal ist es so,

16.2 and sometimes it isn't.
und manchmal nicht.

16.3 You never can tell with paw- marks."
Bei Pfotenabdrücken kann man das nie wissen."

17.1 With these few words he went on tracking, and Piglet,
after watching him for a minute or two, ran after
him.
Mit diesen Worten setzte er seine Spur fort, und Ferkel,
das ihm ein oder zwei Minuten lang nachschaute, lief ihm
nach.

17.2 Winnie-the-Pooh had come to a sudden stop, and was
bending over the tracks in a puzzled sort of way.
Winnie-the-Pooh war plötzlich stehen geblieben und
beugte sich verwirrt über die Schienen.

18.1 "What's the matter?" asked Piglet.
"Was ist denn los?" fragte Ferkel.

19.1 "It's a very funny thing," said Bear,
"Es ist sehr komisch," sagte Bär,

19.2 "but there seem to be two animals now. This -
"aber es scheinen jetzt zwei Tiere zu sein. Dieses -

whatever-it-was - has been joined by another - 19.3

was auch immer es war - hat sich mit einem anderen -

whatever-it- is - 19.4

was auch immer es ist -

and the two of them are now proceeding in company. 19.5

zusammengetan, und die beiden gehen jetzt gemeinsam
weiter.

Would you mind coming with me, Piglet, in case they 19.6
turn out to be Hostile Animals?"

Würdest du bitte mit mir kommen, Ferkel, falls sie sich als
feindliche Tiere herausstellen?"

Piglet scratched his ear in a nice sort of way, and said 20.1
that he had nothing to do until Friday, and would be
delighted to come, in case it really was a Woozle.

Ferkel kratzte sich freundlich am Ohr und sagte, dass er bis
Freitag nichts zu tun habe und gerne kommen würde, falls
es wirklich ein Woozle sei.

"You mean, in case it really is two Woozles," 21.1

"Du meinst, falls es wirklich zwei Woozles sind,"

said Winnie-the-Pooh, and Piglet said that anyhow he 21.2
had nothing to do until Friday.

sagte Winnie-the-Pooh, und Ferkel sagte, dass er bis Freitag
sowieso nichts zu tun habe.

So off they went together. 21.3

Also gingen sie zusammen los.

There was a small spinney of larch trees just here, 23.1
and it seemed as if the two Woozles, if that is what
they were, had been going round this spinney; so
round this spinney went Pooh and Piglet after them;
Piglet passing the time by telling Pooh what his
Grandfather Trespassers W had done to Remove
Stiffness after Tracking, and how his Grandfather
Trespassers W had suffered in his later years from
Shortness of Breath, and other matters of interest,
and Pooh wondering what a Grandfather was like,
and if perhaps this was Two Grandfathers they were
after now, and, if so, whether he would be allowed
to take one home and keep it, and what Christopher
Robin would say.

Hier gab es eine kleine Lärchenallee, und es schien, als ob
die beiden Woozles, wenn sie denn welche waren, um diese
Lärchenallee herumgelaufen wären, und so liefen Puuh
und Ferkel ihnen hinterher; Ferkel vertrieb sich die Zeit,
indem es Puuh erzählte, was sein Großvater Trespassers
W. getan hatte, um die Steifheit nach dem Tracking zu
beseitigen, und wie sein Großvater Trespassers W. in
seinen späteren Jahren an Kurzatmigkeit gelitten hatte,
und andere interessante Dinge, und Puuh fragte sich, wie
ein Großvater wohl sei, und ob es vielleicht zwei Großväter
waren, hinter denen sie jetzt her waren, und wenn ja, ob er
einen mit nach Hause nehmen und behalten dürfte, und
was Christopher Robin dazu sagen würde.

And still the tracks went on in front of them ... 23.2

Und immer noch gingen die Spuren vor ihnen weiter ...

Suddenly Winnie-the-Pooh stopped, and pointed 24.1
excitedly in front of him.

Plötzlich blieb Winnie-the-Pooh stehen und zeigte
aufgeregt vor sich hin.

24.2 **"Look!"**
"Schau!"

25.1 **"What?" said Piglet, with a jump.**
"Was?" sagte Ferkel mit einem Sprung.

25.2 **And then, to show that he hadn't been frightened,
he jumped up and down once or twice more in an
exercising sort of way.**
Und um zu zeigen, dass es sich nicht erschreckt hatte,
hüpfte es noch ein - oder zweimal auf und ab, wie bei einer
Übung.

27.1 **"The tracks!" said Pooh.**
"Die Spuren!" sagte Puuh.

27.2 **"A third animal has joined the other two!"**
"Ein drittes Tier hat sich zu den beiden anderen gesellt!"

28.1 **"Pooh!" cried Piglet. "Do you think it is another
Woozle?"**
"Puuh!" rief Ferkel. "Meinst du, es ist noch ein Woozle?"

29.1 **"No," said Pooh, "because it makes different marks.**
"Nein," sagte Pooh, "denn es macht verschiedene Zeichen.

It is either Two Woozles and one, as it might be,   29.2
Wizzle, or Two, as it might be, Wizzles and one, if
so it is, Woozle.

Entweder sind es zwei Woozles und ein, wie es sein könnte,
Wizzle, oder zwei, wie es sein könnte, Wizzles und ein,
wenn es so ist, Woozle.

Let us continue to follow them."   29.3

Lasst uns ihnen weiter folgen."

So they went on, feeling just a little anxious now,   30.1
in case the three animals in front of them were of
Hostile Intent.

So gingen sie weiter, nur ein wenig ängstlich, für den Fall,
dass die drei Tiere vor ihnen feindliche Absichten hatten.

And Piglet wished very much that his Grandfather   30.2
T. W. were there, instead of elsewhere, and Pooh
thought how nice it would be if they met Christopher
Robin suddenly but quite accidentally, and only
because he liked Christopher Robin so much.

Und Ferkel wünschte sich sehr, dass sein Großvater T. W.
dort wäre und nicht woanders, und Puuh dachte, wie schön
es wäre, wenn sie plötzlich, aber ganz zufällig, Christopher
Robin treffen würden, und das nur, weil er Christopher
Robin so sehr mochte.

And then, all of a sudden, Winnie-the-Pooh stopped   30.3
again, and licked the tip of his nose in a cooling
manner, for he was feeling more hot and anxious
than ever in his life before.

Und dann blieb Winnie-the-Pooh plötzlich wieder stehen
und leckte sich kühlend über die Nasenspitze, denn er
fühlte sich so heiß und ängstlich wie nie zuvor in seinem
Leben.

30.4 There were four animals in front of them!

Da waren vier Tiere vor ihnen!

31.1 "Do you see, Piglet? Look at their tracks!

"Siehst du, Ferkel? Sieh dir ihre Spuren an!

31.2 Three, as it were, Woozles, and one, as it was, Wizzle.

Drei Woozles, sozusagen, und ein Wizzle, sozusagen.

31.3 Another Woozle has joined them!"

Ein weiterer Woozle hat sich ihnen angeschlossen!"

32.1 And so it seemed to be.

Und so schien es auch zu sein.

32.2 There were the tracks; crossing over each other here,
getting muddled up with each other there; but, quite
plainly every now and then, the tracks of four sets of
paws.

Da waren die Spuren, die sich hier kreuzten, dort
durcheinander gerieten, aber immer wieder ganz deutlich
die Spuren von vier Pfotenpaaren.

34.1 "I think,"

"Ich glaube,"

said Piglet, when he had licked the tip of his nose too, and found that it brought very little comfort,

34.2

sagte Ferkel, nachdem es sich auch die Nasenspitze geleckt hatte und feststellte, dass dies nur wenig Trost spendete,

"I think that I have just remembered something.

34.3

"ich glaube, ich habe mich gerade an etwas erinnert.

I have just remembered something that I forgot to do yesterday and shan't be able to do to-morrow.

34.4

Mir ist gerade etwas eingefallen, was ich gestern vergessen habe zu tun und morgen nicht mehr tun können werde.

So I suppose I really ought to go back and do it now."

34.5

Also sollte ich es wohl jetzt nachholen."

"We'll do it this afternoon, and I'll come with you,"

35.1

"Wir machen es heute Nachmittag, und ich komme mit,"

said Pooh.

35.2

sagte Puuh.

"It isn't the sort of thing you can do in the afternoon,"

36.1

"So etwas kann man nicht am Nachmittag machen,"

said Piglet quickly.

36.2

sagte Ferkel schnell.

"It's a very particular morning thing, that has to be done in the morning, and, if possible, between the hours of —— What would you say the time was?"

36.3

"Es ist eine ganz besondere Morgensache, die man morgens machen muss, und zwar möglichst zwischen ...Was würdest du sagen, wie spät es war?"

37.1 "About twelve,"

"Etwa zwölf,"

37.2 said Winnie-the-Pooh, looking at the sun.

sagte Winnie-the-Pooh und schaute in die Sonne.

38.1 "Between, as I was saying, the hours of twelve and
twelve five.

"Zwischen, wie ich schon sagte, zwölf und zwölf Uhr fünf.

38.2 So, really, dear old Pooh, if you'll excuse me ——
What's that?"

Also wirklich, lieber alter Pooh, wenn du mich
entschuldigst ...Was ist das?"

39.1 Pooh looked up at the sky, and then, as he heard the
whistle again, he looked up into the branches of a big
oak-tree, and then he saw a friend of his.

Puuh schaute zum Himmel hinauf, und dann, als er wieder
das Pfeifen hörte, schaute er hinauf in die Äste einer
großen Eiche, und dann sah er seinen Freund.

"It's Christopher Robin," he said.   41.1
"Es ist Christopher Robin," sagte er.

"Ah, then you'll be all right," said Piglet.   42.1
"Ah, dann wird es dir gut gehen," sagte Ferkel.

"You'll be quite safe with him. Good- bye,"   42.2
"Bei ihm bist du in Sicherheit. Auf Wiedersehen,"

and he trotted off home as quickly as he could, very   42.3
glad to be Out of All Danger again.
und er trottete so schnell er konnte nach Hause, froh,
wieder außer Gefahr zu sein.

Christopher Robin came slowly down his tree.   44.1
Christopher Robin kam langsam von seinem Baum
herunter.

"Silly old Bear," he said, "what were you doing?   45.1
"Dummer alter Bär," sagte er, "was hast du denn gemacht?

45.2 First you went round the spinney twice by yourself, and then Piglet ran after you and you went round again together, and then you were just going round a fourth time —— "

Erst bist du zweimal allein um die Spinnerei gelaufen, dann ist Ferkel hinter dir hergelaufen, und ihr seid noch einmal zusammen um die Spinnerei gelaufen, und dann wolltest du gerade ein viertes Mal um die Spinnerei laufen ..."

46.1 "Wait a moment,"

"Warte einen Moment,"

46.2 said Winnie-the-Pooh, holding up his paw.

sagte Winnie-the-Pooh und hielt seine Pfote hoch.

47.1 He sat down and thought, in the most thoughtful way he could think.

Er setzte sich hin und dachte nach, und zwar auf die nachdenklichste Weise, die er denken konnte.

47.2 Then he fitted his paw into one of the Tracks ...

Dann steckte er seine Pfote in einen der Tracks ...

47.3 and then he scratched his nose twice, and stood up.

und dann kratzte er sich zweimal an der Nase und stand auf.

48.1 "Yes," said Winnie-the-Pooh.

"Ja," sagte Winnie-the-Pooh.

49.1 "I see now," said Winnie-the-Pooh.

"Jetzt verstehe ich," sagte Winnie-the-Pooh.

50.1 "I have been Foolish and Deluded," said he,

"Ich war töricht und habe mich getäuscht," sagte er,

"and I am a Bear of No Brain at All." 50.2

"und ich bin ein Bär ohne Hirn."

"You're the Best Bear in All the World," 51.1

"Du bist der beste Bär auf der ganzen Welt,"

said Christopher Robin soothingly. 51.2

sagte Christopher Robin beruhigend.

"Am I?" said Pooh hopefully. 52.1

"Bin ich das?" sagte Pooh hoffnungsvoll.

And then he brightened up suddenly. 52.2

Und dann erhellte er sich plötzlich.

"Anyhow," he said, "it is nearly Luncheon Time." 53.1

"Wie auch immer," sagte er, "es ist fast Essenszeit."

So he went home for it. 54.1

Also ging er dafür nach Hause.

CHAPTER IV · IN WHICH EEYORE LOSES A TAIL AND POOH FINDS ONE

KAPITEL IV · IN DEM EEYORE EINEN
SCHWANZ VERLIERT UND POOH EINEN
FINDET

1.1 The Old Grey Donkey, Eeyore, stood by himself in a
thistly corner of the forest, his front feet well apart,
his head on one side, and thought about things.
Der alte graue Esel, I-Aah, stand allein in einer schattigen
Ecke des Waldes, die Vorderfüße weit auseinander, den
Kopf auf einer Seite, und dachte über Dinge nach.

1.2 Sometimes he thought sadly to himself, "Why?"
Manchmal dachte er traurig, "Warum?"

1.3 and sometimes he thought, "Wherefore?"
und manchmal dachte er, "Wozu?"

1.4 and sometimes he thought, "Inasmuch as which?"
und manchmal dachte er, "Worüber denn?"

– and sometimes he didn't quite know what he was
thinking about.

1.5

– und manchmal wusste er nicht recht, worüber er
nachdachte.

So when Winnie-the-Pooh came stumping along,
Eeyore was very glad to be able to stop thinking for a
little, in order to say,

1.6

Als dann Winnie-the-Pooh daherkam, war I-Aah sehr froh,
dass er ein wenig aufhören konnte zu denken, um ihm zu
sagen,

"How do you do?" in a gloomy manner to him.

1.7

"Wie geht es Ihnen?" mit düsterer Miene.

"And how are you?" said Winnie-the-Pooh.

3.1

"Und wie geht es dir?" fragte Winnie-the-Pooh.

Eeyore shook his head from side to side.

4.1

I-Aah schüttelte den Kopf hin und her.

"Not very how," he said.

5.1

"Nicht sehr wie," sagte er.

74

5.2 **"I don't seem to have felt at all how for a long time."**
"Ich glaube, ich habe schon lange nicht mehr gespürt, wie."

6.1 **"Dear, dear," said Pooh, "I'm sorry about that.**
"Oje, oje," sagte Puuh, "das tut mir aber leid.

6.2 **Let's have a look at you."**
Lass dich mal anschauen."

7.1 **So Eeyore stood there, gazing sadly at the ground,
and Winnie-the-Pooh walked all round him once.**
So stand I-Aah da und starrte traurig auf den Boden, und
Winnie Puuh ging einmal um ihn herum.

9.1 **"Why, what's happened to your tail?" he said in
surprise.**
"Was ist denn mit deinem Schwanz passiert?" fragte er
erstaunt.

10.1 **"What has happened to it?" said Eeyore.**
"Was ist damit passiert?" fragte I-Aah.

11.1 **"It isn't there!"**
"Es ist nicht da!"

"Are you sure?"   12.1
"Sind Sie sicher?"

"Well, either a tail is there or it isn't there.   13.1
"Nun, entweder ist ein Schwanz da oder nicht.

You can't make a mistake about it. And yours isn't   13.2
there!"
Da kann man sich nicht irren. Und deiner ist nicht da!"

"Then what is?"   14.1
"Was ist es dann?"

"Nothing."   15.1
"Nichts."

"Let's have a look,"   17.1
"Lass uns nachsehen,"

76

17.2 said Eeyore, and he turned slowly round to the place
where his tail had been a little while ago, and then,
finding that he couldn't catch it up, he turned round
the other way, until he came back to where he was
at first, and then he put his head down and looked
between his front legs, and at last he said, with a long,
sad sigh,

sagte I-Aah, und er drehte sich langsam zu der Stelle um,
an der sein Schwanz vorhin gewesen war, und dann, als er
merkte, dass er ihn nicht einholen konnte, drehte er sich
in die andere Richtung, bis er wieder an der Stelle war, an
der er zuerst war, und dann legte er den Kopf in den Nacken
und schaute zwischen seine Vorderbeine, und schließlich
sagte er mit einem langen, traurigen Seufzer,

17.3 "I believe you're right."

"Ich glaube, du hast recht."

18.1 "Of course I'm right," said Pooh.

"Natürlich habe ich Recht," sagte Pooh.

19.1 "That Accounts for a Good Deal," said Eeyore
gloomily.

"Das macht eine ganze Menge aus," sagte I-Aah düster.

19.2 "It Explains Everything. No Wonder."

"Es erklärt alles. Kein Wunder."

20.1 "You must have left it somewhere,"

"Du musst es irgendwo liegen gelassen haben,"

20.2 said Winnie-the-Pooh.

sagte Winnie-the-Pooh.

"Somebody must have taken it," said Eeyore. 21.1

"Jemand muss es genommen haben," sagte I-Aah.

"How Like Them," he added, after a long silence. 21.2

"So wie sie," fügte er nach langem Schweigen hinzu.

Pooh felt that he ought to say something helpful 23.1
about it, but didn't quite know what.

Puuh hatte das Gefühl, dass er etwas Hilfreiches dazu sagen
sollte, aber er wusste nicht so recht, was.

So he decided to do something helpful instead. 23.2

Also beschloss er, stattdessen etwas Hilfreiches zu tun.

"Eeyore," he said solemnly, 24.1

"I-Aah," sagte er feierlich,

"I, Winnie-the-Pooh, will find your tail for you." 24.2

"ich, Winnie-the-Pooh, werde deinen Schwanz für dich
finden."

"Thank you, Pooh," answered Eeyore. 25.1

"Danke, Puuh," antwortete I-Aah.

"You're a real friend," said he. "Not like Some," 25.2

"Du bist ein echter Freund," sagte er. "Nicht wie manche,"

25.3 **he said.**

sagte er.

26.1 **So Winnie-the-Pooh went off to find Eeyore's tail.**

Also machte sich Winnie-the-Pooh auf den Weg, um I-Aahs
Schwanz zu finden.

27.1 **It was a fine spring morning in the forest as he started
out.**

Es war ein schöner Frühlingsmorgen im Wald, als er
aufbrach.

27.2 **Little soft clouds played happily in a blue sky,
skipping from time to time in front of the sun as if
they had come to put it out, and then sliding away
suddenly so that the next might have his turn.**

Kleine weiche Wölkchen spielten fröhlich am blauen
Himmel, hüpften von Zeit zu Zeit vor der Sonne her, als
wollten sie sie auslöschen, und schoben sich dann plötzlich
weg, damit die nächste an die Reihe kommen konnte.

27.3 **Through them and between them the sun shone
bravely; and a copse which had worn its firs all the
year round seemed old and dowdy now beside the
new green lace which the beeches had put on so
prettily.**

Durch sie hindurch und zwischen ihnen hindurch schien
die Sonne tapfer, und ein Wäldchen, das das ganze Jahr
über seine Tannen getragen hatte, wirkte jetzt alt und
schäbig neben den neuen grünen Spitzen, die die Buchen so
hübsch angelegt hatten.

Through copse and spinney marched Bear; down 27.4
open slopes of gorse and heather, over rocky beds
of streams, up steep banks of sandstone into the
heather again; and so at last, tired and hungry, to the
Hundred Acre Wood.

Durch Wäldchen und Feldgehölze marschierte Bear, über
offene Hänge mit Ginster und Heidekraut, über felsige
Bachbetten, steile Sandsteinbänke hinauf, wieder ins
Heidekraut, und so erreichte er schließlich, müde und
hungrig, den Hundertmorgenwald.

For it was in the Hundred Acre Wood that Owl lived. 27.5

Denn im Hundertmorgenwald lebte die Eule.

"And if anyone knows anything about anything," 28.1

"Und wenn jemand etwas über irgendetwas weiß,"

said Bear to himself, 28.2

sagte Bär zu sich selbst,

"it's Owl who knows something about something," 28.3
he said,

"dann ist es Eule, die etwas über etwas weiß," sagte er,

"or my name's not Winnie-the-Pooh," he said. 28.4

"oder mein Name ist nicht Winnie-the-Pooh," sagte er.

"Which it is," he added. "So there you are." 28.5

"Und das ist er," fügte er hinzu. "Da bist du also."

29.1 Owl lived at The Chestnuts, an old-world residence of
great charm, which was grander than anybody else's,
or seemed so to Bear, because it had both a knocker
and a bell-pull.

Eule wohnte in "The Chestnuts," einem altmodischen Haus
von großem Charme, das größer war als alle anderen, oder
das Bear so erschien, weil es sowohl einen Türklopfer als
auch einen Klingelzug hatte.

29.2 Underneath the knocker there was a notice which
said:

Unter dem Türklopfer befand sich ein Zettel, auf dem
stand:

30.1 PLES RING IF AN RNSER IS REQIRD.

BITTE RUFEN SIE AN, WENN SIE EINE PERSON
BENÖTIGEN.

31.1 Underneath the bell-pull there was a notice which
said:

Unter dem Klingelzug befand sich ein Zettel mit der
Aufschrift:

32.1 PLEZ CNOKE IF AN RNSR IS NOT REQID.

BITTE FRAGEN SIE NACH, WENN SIE KEINE
GENEHMIGUNG BENÖTIGEN.

These notices had been written by Christopher Robin,

34.1

Diese Zettel waren von Christopher Robin geschrieben worden,

who was the only one in the forest who could spell;

34.2

der als einziger im Wald buchstabieren konnte;

for Owl, wise though he was in many ways, able to read and write and spell his own name WOL, yet somehow went all to pieces over delicate words like MEASLES and BUTTEREDTOAST.

34.3

denn Eule, obwohl er in vielerlei Hinsicht weise war, lesen und schreiben und seinen eigenen Namen WOL buchstabieren konnte, kam bei so heiklen Wörtern wie MEASELN und BUTTEREDTOAST irgendwie durcheinander.

35.1 Winnie-the-Pooh read the two notices very carefully,
first from left to right, and afterwards, in case he had
missed some of it, from right to left.

Winnie-the-Pooh las die beiden Zettel sehr sorgfältig,
zuerst von links nach rechts und dann, falls er etwas
übersehen hatte, von rechts nach links.

35.2 Then, to make quite sure, he knocked and pulled the
knocker, and he pulled and knocked the bell-rope,
and he called out in a very loud voice,

Dann klopfte er, um ganz sicher zu gehen, und zog am
Türklopfer, und er zog und klopfte an der Klingelschnur,
und er rief mit sehr lauter Stimme,

35.3 "Owl! I require an answer! It's Bear speaking."

"Eule! Ich brauche eine Antwort! Hier spricht der Bär."

35.4 And the door opened, and Owl looked out.

Die Tür öffnete sich, und Eule schaute hinaus.

36.1 "Hallo, Pooh," he said. "How's things?"

"Hallo, Pooh," sagte er. "Wie geht's?"

37.1 "Terrible and Sad," said Pooh,

"Schrecklich und traurig," sagte Puuh,

37.2 "because Eeyore, who is a friend of mine, has lost his
tail.

"weil I-Aah, der ein Freund von mir ist, seinen Schwanz
verloren hat.

37.3 And he's Moping about it.

Und er bläst deswegen Trübsal.

So could you very kindly tell me how to find it for him?"

37.4

Könntest du mir also freundlicherweise sagen, wie ich ihn für ihn finden kann?"

"Well," said Owl,

38.1

"Nun," sagte Eule,

"the customary procedure in such cases is as follows."

38.2

"die übliche Vorgehensweise in solchen Fällen ist wie folgt."

"What does Crustimoney Proseedcake mean?" said Pooh.

39.1

"Was bedeutet Krustenwurzelkuchen?" fragte Puuh.

"For I am a Bear of Very Little Brain,

39.2

"Denn ich bin ein Bär mit sehr wenig Hirn,

and long words Bother me."

39.3

und lange Wörter stören mich."

"It means the Thing to Do."

40.1

"Es bedeutet das, was zu tun ist."

"As long as it means that, I don't mind,"

41.1

"Solange es das bedeutet, macht es mir nichts aus,"

said Pooh humbly.

41.2

sagte Pooh bescheiden.

"The thing to do is as follows. First, Issue a Reward.

42.1

"Das Vorgehen ist wie folgt. Erstens, gib eine Belohnung aus.

42.2 Then —— "
Dann ..."

43.1 "Just a moment," said Pooh, holding up his paw.
"Einen Moment," sagte Pooh und hielt seine Pfote hoch.

43.2 "What do we do to this — what you were saying?
"Was machen wir mit dem, was du gerade gesagt hast?

43.3 You sneezed just as you were going to tell me."
Du hast geniest, gerade als du es mir sagen wolltest."

44.1 "I didn't sneeze."
"Ich habe nicht geniest."

45.1 "Yes, you did, Owl."
"Ja, das hast du, Eule."

46.1 "Excuse me, Pooh, I didn't.
"Entschuldige, Puuh, ich habe nicht geniest.

46.2 You can't sneeze without knowing it."
Man kann nicht niesen, ohne es zu wissen."

47.1 "Well, you can't know it without something having been sneezed."
"Nun, man kann es nicht wissen, ohne dass man etwas geniest hat."

48.1 "What I said was, 'First Issue a Reward'."
"Ich habe gesagt, 'Gib zuerst eine Belohnung aus'."

"You're doing it again," said Pooh sadly. 49.1

"Du tust es schon wieder," sagte Pooh traurig.

"A Reward!" said Owl very loudly. 50.1

"Eine Belohnung!" sagte Eule sehr laut.

"We write a notice to say that we will give a large 50.2
something to anybody who finds Eeyore's tail."

"Wir schreiben einen Zettel, auf dem steht, dass wir
demjenigen, der I-Aahs Schwanz findet, eine große
Belohnung geben werden."

"I see, I see," 52.1

"Ich verstehe, ich verstehe,"

said Pooh, nodding his head. 52.2

sagte Pooh und nickte mit dem Kopf.

"Talking about large somethings," 52.3

"Da wir gerade von großen Dingen sprechen,"

he went on dreamily, 52.4

fuhr er verträumt fort,

52.5 "I generally have a small something about now —
about this time in the morning,"
"ich habe normalerweise eine Kleinigkeit zu mir
genommen — ungefähr um diese Zeit am Morgen,"

52.6 and he looked wistfully at the cupboard in the corner
of Owl's parlour;
und er blickte wehmütig auf den Schrank in der Ecke von
Eulens Stube;

52.7 "just a mouthful of condensed milk or whatnot,
"nur einen Schluck Kondensmilch oder so etwas,

52.8 with perhaps a lick of honey —— "
vielleicht mit einem Klecks Honig —— "

53.1 "Well, then," said Owl,
"Nun, dann," sagte Eule,

53.2 we write out this notice, and we put it up all over the
forest."
"schreiben wir diesen Zettel und hängen ihn überall im
Wald auf."

54.1 "A lick of honey," murmured Bear to himself,
"Ein bisschen Honig," murmelte Bär vor sich hin,

54.2 "or — or not, as the case may be."
"oder auch nicht, je nachdem."

54.3 And he gave a deep sigh,
Er stieß einen tiefen Seufzer aus und bemühte sich sehr,

54.4 and tried very hard to listen to what Owl was saying.
Eule zuzuhören.

But Owl went on and on, using longer and longer
words, until at last he came back to where he started,
and he explained that the person to write out this
notice was Christopher Robin.

55.1

Aber die Eule redete immer weiter, benutzte immer längere
Wörter, bis sie schließlich zu ihrem Ausgangspunkt
zurückkam und erklärte, dass derjenige, der diesen Zettel
ausfüllen sollte, Christopher Robin war.

"It was he who wrote the ones on my front
door for me.

56.1

"Er war es, der die Zettel an meiner Haustür für mich
geschrieben hat.

Did you see them, Pooh?"

56.2

Hast du sie gesehen, Puuh?"

For some time now Pooh had been saying

57.1

Seit einiger Zeit sagte Pooh mit geschlossenen Augen
abwechselnd

"Yes" and "No"

57.2

"Ja" und "Nein"

in turn, with his eyes shut, to all that Owl was saying,
and having said,

57.3

zu allem, was Eule sagte, und nachdem er beim letzten Mal,

"Yes, yes," last time, he said "No, not at all,"

57.4

"Ja, ja" gesagt hatte, sagte er jetzt "Nein, überhaupt nicht,"

now, without really knowing what Owl was talking
about.

57.5

ohne wirklich zu wissen, wovon Eule sprach.

58.1 "Didn't you see them?" said Owl, a little surprised.

"Hast du sie nicht gesehen?" sagte Eule ein wenig überrascht.

58.2 "Come and look at them now."

"Komm und sieh sie dir jetzt an."

59.1 So they went outside.

Also gingen sie nach draußen.

59.2 And Pooh looked at the knocker and the notice below it, and he looked at the bell-rope and the notice below it, and the more he looked at the bell-rope, the more he felt that he had seen something like it, somewhere else, sometime before.

Und Puuh schaute auf den Türklopfer und den Zettel darunter, und er schaute auf den Klingelstrang und den Zettel darunter, und je mehr er auf den Klingelstrang schaute, desto mehr fühlte er, dass er etwas Ähnliches schon einmal irgendwo anders gesehen hatte, irgendwann einmal.

60.1 "Handsome bell-rope, isn't it?" said Owl.

"Ein hübsches Glockenseil, nicht wahr?" sagte Eule.

61.1 Pooh nodded.

Puuh nickte.

62.1 "It reminds me of something," he said,

"Es erinnert mich an etwas," sagte er,

62.2 "but I can't think what. Where did you get it?"

"aber ich weiß nicht, an was. Woher hast du es?"

"I just came across it in the Forest.   64.1

"Ich habe es gerade im Wald gefunden.

It was hanging over a bush, and I thought at first   64.2
somebody lived there, so I rang it, and nothing
happened, and then I rang it again very loudly, and it
came off in my hand, and as nobody seemed to want
it, I took it home, and —— "

Es hing über einem Busch, und ich dachte zuerst, dass dort
jemand wohnt, also läutete ich es, und es passierte nichts,
und dann läutete ich es noch einmal sehr laut, und es löste
sich in meiner Hand, und da es niemand zu wollen schien,
nahm ich es mit nach Hause, und ..."

"Owl," said Pooh solemnly,   65.1

"Eule," sagte Puuh feierlich,

"you made a mistake. Somebody did want it."   65.2

"du hast einen Fehler gemacht. Jemand hat es gewollt."

66.1 "Who?"
"Wer?"

67.1 "Eeyore. My dear friend Eeyore. He was — he was
fond of it."
"I-Aah. Mein lieber Freund I-Aah. Er war — er mochte es."

68.1 "Fond of it?"
"Mögen Sie es?"

69.1 "Attached to it," said Winnie-the-Pooh sadly.
"Daran hängen," sagte Winnie-the-Pooh traurig.

So with these words he unhooked it, and carried it   71.1
back to Eeyore; and when Christopher Robin had
nailed it on in its right place again, Eeyore frisked
about the forest, waving his tail so happily that
Winnie-the-Pooh came over all funny, and had to
hurry home for a little snack of something to sustain
him.

Mit diesen Worten löste er den Haken und trug ihn zurück
zu I-Aah, und als Christopher Robin ihn wieder an der
richtigen Stelle festgenagelt hatte, hüpfte I-Aah durch
den Wald und wedelte so fröhlich mit dem Schwanz, dass
Winnie-the-Pooh ganz komisch wurde und nach Hause
eilen musste, um eine Kleinigkeit zu essen, die ihn stärkte.

And, wiping his mouth half an hour afterwards, he   71.2
sang to himself proudly:

Und als er sich eine halbe Stunde später den Mund
abwischte, sang er stolz vor sich hin:

Who found the Tail?   72.1

Wer hat den Schwanz gefunden?

"I," said Pooh,   73.1

"Ich," sagte Puuh,

"At a quarter to two   74.1

"Um viertel vor zwei

(Only it was quarter to eleven really),   75.1

(Eigentlich war es erst viertel vor elf),

92

— I —

77.1   found the Tail!"
Ich habe den Schwanz gefunden!"

CHAPTER V · IN WHICH PIGLET MEETS A HEFFALUMP

KAPITEL V · IN DER EIN FERKEL AUF EINE HEFFALUMP TRIFFT

1.1 One day, when Christopher Robin and Winnie-the-Pooh and Piglet were all talking together, Christopher Robin finished the mouthful he was eating and said carelessly:

Eines Tages, als Christopher Robin, Winnie-the-Pooh und Ferkel miteinander sprachen, beendete Christopher Robin den Bissen, den er gerade aß, und sagte achtlos:

1.2 "I saw a Heffalump to-day, Piglet."

"Ich habe heute einen Heffalump gesehen, Ferkel."

2.1 "What was it doing?" asked Piglet.

"Was hat es gemacht?" fragte Ferkel.

3.1 "Just lumping along," said Christopher Robin.

"Ich bin nur so dahingeplumpst," sagte Christopher Robin.

"I don't think it saw me." 3.2
"Ich glaube, es hat mich nicht gesehen."

"I saw one once," said Piglet. 4.1
"Ich habe einmal einen gesehen," sagte Ferkel.

"At least, I think I did," he said. 4.2
"Zumindest glaube ich das," sagte er.

"Only perhaps it wasn't." 4.3
"Aber vielleicht war es auch keiner."

"So did I," said Pooh, 5.1
"Ich auch," sagte Pooh und fragte sich,

wondering what a Heffalump was like. 5.2
wie ein Heffalump aussieht.

**"You don't often see them," said Christopher Robin
carelessly.** 6.1
"Man sieht sie nicht oft," sagte Christopher Robin achtlos.

"Not now," said Piglet. 7.1
"Nicht jetzt," sagte Ferkel.

"Not at this time of year," said Pooh. 8.1
"Nicht zu dieser Jahreszeit," sagte Pooh.

10.1 Then they all talked about something else, until it was time for Pooh and Piglet to go home together.

Dann unterhielten sie sich über etwas anderes, bis es Zeit für Puuh und Ferkel war, gemeinsam nach Hause zu gehen.

10.2 At first as they stumped along the path which edged the Hundred Acre Wood,

Als sie den Pfad am Rande des Hundertmorgenwaldes entlang stapften,

10.3 they didn't say much to each other;

sagten sie zunächst nicht viel zueinander;

10.4 but when they came to the stream and had helped each other across the stepping stones, and were able to walk side by side again over the heather, they began to talk in a friendly way about this and that, and Piglet said,

Aber als sie an den Bach kamen und sich gegenseitig über die Trittsteine geholfen hatten und wieder nebeneinander über das Heidekraut gehen konnten, begannen sie freundlich über dies und jenes zu reden, und Ferkel sagte,

10.5 "If you see what I mean, Pooh," and Pooh said,

"Wenn du siehst, was ich meine, Puuh," und Puuh sagte,

"It's just what I think myself, Piglet," 10.6
"Das ist genau das, was ich auch denke, Ferkel,"

and Piglet said, 10.7
und Ferkel sagte,

"But, on the other hand, Pooh, we must remember," 10.8
"Aber andererseits, Puuh, müssen wir daran denken,"

and Pooh said, 10.9
und Puuh sagte,

"Quite true, Piglet, although I had forgotten it for the 10.10
moment."
"Ganz recht, Ferkel, auch wenn ich es im Augenblick
vergessen hatte."

And then, just as they came to the Six Pine Trees, 10.11
Pooh looked round to see that nobody else was
listening, and said in a very solemn voice:
Und dann, gerade als sie zu den Sechs Kiefern kamen,
schaute Puuh sich um, um zu sehen, dass niemand sonst
zuhörte, und sagte mit sehr ernster Stimme:

"Piglet, I have decided something." 11.1
"Ferkel, ich habe etwas beschlossen."

"What have you decided, Pooh?" 12.1
"Was hast du entschieden, Pooh?"

"I have decided to catch a Heffalump." 13.1
"Ich habe beschlossen, einen Heffalump zu fangen."

14.1 **Pooh nodded his head several times as he said this, and waited for Piglet to say**

Puuh nickte mehrmals mit dem Kopf, während er dies sagte, und wartete darauf, dass Ferkel

14.2 **"How?" or "Pooh, you couldn't!"**

"Wie?" oder "Puuh, das kannst du nicht!"

14.3 **or something helpful of that sort,**

oder etwas anderes Hilfreiches in dieser Art sagen würde,

14.4 **but Piglet said nothing.**

aber Ferkel sagte nichts.

14.5 **The fact was Piglet was wishing that he had thought about it first.**

Ferkel wünschte sich nämlich, er hätte vorher darüber nachgedacht.

15.1 **"I shall do it,"**

"Ich werde es tun,"

15.2 **said Pooh, after waiting a little longer,**

sagte Puuh, nachdem er ein wenig länger gewartet hatte,

15.3 **"by means of a trap.**

"mit Hilfe einer Falle.

15.4 **And it must be a Cunning Trap, so you will have to help me, Piglet."**

Und es muss eine schlaue Falle sein, also wirst du mir helfen müssen, Ferkel."

16.1 **"Pooh,"**

"Puuh,"

said Piglet, feeling quite happy again now,
16.2
sagte Ferkel, das sich jetzt wieder ganz glücklich fühlte,

"I will." And then he said,
16.3
"das werde ich." Und dann fragte er,

"How shall we do it?" and Pooh said, "That's just it.
16.4
"Wie sollen wir es machen?" und Puuh sagte, "Das ist es ja.

How?"
16.5
Wie?"

And then they sat down together to think it out.
16.6
Und dann setzten sie sich zusammen und überlegten es
sich.

Pooh's first idea was that they should dig a Very Deep
17.1
Pit, and then the Heffalump would come along and
fall into the Pit, and ——
Puuhs erste Idee war, dass sie eine sehr tiefe Grube graben
sollten, und dann würde der Heffalump vorbeikommen
und in die Grube fallen, und ...

"Why?" said Piglet.
18.1
"Warum?" fragte Ferkel.

"Why what?" said Pooh.
19.1
"Warum was?" fragte Puuh.

"Why would he fall in?"
20.1
"Warum sollte er hineinfallen?"

21.1 Pooh rubbed his nose with his paw, and said that the Heffalump might be walking along, humming a little song, and looking up at the sky, wondering if it would rain, and so he wouldn't see the Very Deep Pit until he was half-way down, when it would be too late.

Puuh rieb sich mit seiner Pfote die Nase und sagte, dass der Heffalump vielleicht gerade spazieren ging, ein Liedchen summte und zum Himmel schaute, um zu sehen, ob es regnen würde, und dass er die sehr tiefe Grube erst sehen würde, wenn er schon halb unten war, und dann wäre es zu spät.

22.1 Piglet said that this was a very good Trap, but supposing it were raining already?

Ferkel sagte, das sei eine sehr gute Falle, aber wenn es nun schon regnen würde?

23.1 Pooh rubbed his nose again,

Puuh rieb sich wieder die Nase und sagte,

23.2 and said that he hadn't thought of that.

daran habe er nicht gedacht.

23.3 And then he brightened up, and said that, if it were raining already, the Heffalump would be looking at the sky wondering if it would clear up, and so he wouldn't see the Very Deep Pit until he was half-way down ...When it would be too late.

Dann hellte er sich auf und sagte, wenn es schon regnen würde, würde der Heffalump zum Himmel schauen und sich fragen, ob es aufklart, und so würde er die sehr tiefe Grube erst sehen, wenn er auf halbem Weg nach unten wäre ...Dann würde es zu spät sein.

Piglet said that, now that this point had been
explained, he thought it was a Cunning Trap.

24.1

Ferkel sagte, dass es jetzt, nachdem dieser Punkt erklärt
worden war, dachte, es sei eine schlaue Falle.

Pooh was very proud when he heard this, and he felt
that the Heffalump was as good as caught already,
but there was just one other thing which had to be
thought about, and it was this.

25.1

Puuh war sehr stolz, als er das hörte, und er hatte das
Gefühl, dass der Heffalump schon so gut wie gefangen war,
aber es gab nur noch eine Sache, über die man nachdenken
musste, und das war diese.

Where should they dig the Very Deep Pit?

25.2

Wo sollten sie die sehr tiefe Grube graben?

Piglet said that the best place would be somewhere
where a Heffalump was, just before he fell into it,
only about a foot farther on.

26.1

Ferkel sagte, der beste Platz wäre dort, wo ein Heffalump
war, kurz bevor er hineinfiel, nur etwa einen Meter weiter.

"But then he would see us digging it," said Pooh.

27.1

"Aber dann würde er uns beim Graben sehen," sagte Puuh.

"Not if he was looking at the sky."

28.1

"Nicht, wenn er in den Himmel geschaut hat."

"He would Suspect," said Pooh,

29.1

"Er würde es vermuten," sagte Pooh,

"if he happened to look down."

29.2

"wenn er zufällig nach unten schauen würde."

29.3 He thought for a long time and then added sadly,

Er dachte lange nach und fügte dann traurig hinzu,

29.4 "It isn't as easy as I thought.

"Es ist nicht so einfach, wie ich dachte.

29.5 I suppose that's why Heffalumps hardly ever get caught."

Ich nehme an, deshalb werden Heffalumps fast nie erwischt."

30.1 "That must be it," said Piglet.

"Das muss es sein," sagte Ferkel.

31.1 They sighed and got up; and when they had taken a few gorse prickles out of themselves they sat down again; and all the time Pooh was saying to himself,

Sie seufzten und standen auf; und als sie sich ein paar Ginsterstacheln herausgeholt hatten, setzten sie sich wieder hin, und die ganze Zeit über sagte Puuh zu sich selbst,

31.2 "If only I could think of something!"

"Wenn mir nur etwas einfiele!"

31.3 For he felt sure that a Very Clever Brain could catch a Heffalump if only he knew the right way to go about it.

Denn er war sich sicher, dass ein sehr schlaues Gehirn einen Heffalump fangen könnte, wenn es nur wüsste, wie man es richtig anstellt.

32.1 "Suppose," he said to Piglet, "you wanted to catch me,

"Angenommen," sagte er zu Ferkel, "du willst mich fangen,

how would you do it?"   32.2
wie würdest du es tun?"

"Well," said Piglet, "I should do it like this.   33.1
"Nun," sagte Ferkel, "ich würde es so machen.

I should make a Trap, and I should put a Jar of Honey   33.2
in the Trap, and you would smell it, and you would go
in after it, and —— "
Ich würde eine Falle bauen und ein Glas Honig in die Falle
stellen, und du würdest es riechen, und du würdest hinein
gehen und ..."

"And I would go in after it," said Pooh excitedly,   34.1
"Und ich würde hinterhergehen," sagte Pooh aufgeregt,

"only very carefully so as not to hurt myself, and I   34.2
would get to the Jar of Honey, and I should lick round
the edges first of all, pretending that there wasn't
any more, you know, and then I should walk away
and think about it a little, and then I should come
back and start licking in the middle of the jar, and
then —— "
"nur ganz vorsichtig, um mich nicht zu verletzen, und ich
würde zum Honigglas kommen und zuerst an den Rändern
herumlecken und so tun, als wäre nichts mehr da, weißt du,
und dann würde ich weggehen und ein bisschen darüber
nachdenken, und dann würde ich zurückkommen und in
der Mitte des Glases anfangen zu lecken, und dann ..."

"Yes, well never mind about that. There you   35.1
would be,
"Ja, nun, das ist egal. Dort würdest du sein,

and there I should catch you.   35.2
und dort sollte ich dich erwischen.

104

35.3 Now the first thing to think of is, What do Heffalumps like?

Das erste, woran man denken sollte, ist: Was mögen Heffalumps?

35.4 I should think acorns, shouldn't you?

Ich würde sagen, Eicheln, du nicht?

35.5 We'll get a lot of —— I say, wake up, Pooh!"

Wir werden eine Menge ...Wach auf, Puuh!"

36.1 Pooh, who had gone into a happy dream, woke up with a start, and said that Honey was a much more trappy thing than Haycorns.

Puuh, der in einen glücklichen Traum versunken war, wachte mit einem Schreck auf und sagte, dass Honig eine viel gefährlichere Falle sei als Heukörner.

36.2 Piglet didn't think so; and they were just going to argue about it, when Piglet remembered that, if they put acorns in the Trap, he would have to find the acorns, but if they put honey, then Pooh would have to give up some of his own honey, so he said,

Ferkel war anderer Meinung, und sie wollten sich gerade darüber streiten, als Ferkel sich erinnerte, dass, wenn sie Eicheln in die Falle legten, er die Eicheln suchen musste, aber wenn sie Honig legten, musste Puuh etwas von seinem eigenen Honig abgeben, und so sagte er,

36.3 "All right, honey then,"

"Na gut, dann eben Honig,"

36.4 just as Pooh remembered it too, and was going to say,

gerade als Puuh sich auch daran erinnerte und sagen wollte,

"All right, haycorns." 36.5

"Na gut, Heuhörner."

"Honey," said Piglet to himself in a thoughtful way, 37.1

"Honig," sagte Ferkel nachdenklich zu sich selbst,

as if it were now settled. 37.2

als ob die Sache nun entschieden wäre.

"I'll dig the pit, while you go and get the honey." 37.3

"Ich werde die Grube graben, während du den Honig
holst."

"Very well," said Pooh, and he stumped off. 38.1

"Nun gut," sagte Pooh und stapfte davon.

40.1 As soon as he got home, he went to the larder; and he stood on a chair, and took down a very large jar of honey from the top shelf.

Sobald er nach Hause kam, ging er in die Speisekammer, stellte sich auf einen Stuhl und nahm ein großes Glas Honig aus dem obersten Regal.

40.2 It had HUNNY written on it, but, just to make sure, he took off the paper cover and looked at it, and it looked just like honey.

Auf dem Glas stand HUNNY, aber um sicherzugehen, nahm er den Papierdeckel ab und sah es sich an, und es sah genau wie Honig aus.

40.3 "But you never can tell," said Pooh.

"Aber man kann nie wissen," sagte Pooh.

40.4 "I remember my uncle saying once that he had seen cheese just this colour."

"Ich erinnere mich, dass mein Onkel einmal gesagt hat, dass er Käse mit genau dieser Farbe gesehen hat."

40.5 So he put his tongue in, and took a large lick.

Also steckte er seine Zunge hinein und leckte kräftig daran.

40.6 "Yes," he said, "it is.

"Ja," sagte er, "das ist er.

40.7 No doubt about that.

Daran besteht kein Zweifel.

40.8 And honey, I should say, right down to the bottom of the jar.

Und Honig, würde ich sagen, bis auf den Boden des Glases.

40.9 Unless, of course," he said,

Es sei denn," sagte er,

"somebody put cheese in at the bottom just for a joke. 40.10
"jemand hat aus Jux und Tollerei unten Käse reingetan.

Perhaps I had better go a little further ... 40.11
Vielleicht sollte ich noch ein bisschen weiter gehen ...

just in case ... 40.12
nur für den Fall ...

in case Heffalumps don't like cheese ... 40.13
für den Fall, dass Heffalumps keinen Käse mögen ...

same as me ...Ah!" And he gave a deep sigh. 40.14
genau wie ich ...Ah!" Und er stieß einen tiefen Seufzer aus.

"I was right. It is honey, right the way down." 40.15
"Ich hatte recht. Es ist Honig, bis ganz nach unten."

Having made certain of this, he took the jar back to 42.1
Piglet, and Piglet looked up from the bottom of his
Very Deep Pit, and said,
Als er sich vergewissert hatte, brachte er den Krug zurück
zu Ferkel, und Ferkel schaute vom Grund seiner sehr tiefen
Grube auf und fragte,

42.2 "Got it?" and Pooh said,
"Hast du ihn?" und Puuh sagte,

42.3 "Yes, but it isn't quite a full jar,"
"Ja, aber er ist nicht ganz voll,"

42.4 and he threw it down to Piglet, and Piglet said, "No,
und er warf ihn zu Ferkel hinunter, und Ferkel sagte,
"Nein,

42.5 it isn't! Is that all you've got left?"
das ist er nicht! Ist das alles, was du noch hast?"

42.6 and Pooh said "Yes." Because it was.
und Puuh sagte, "Ja." Weil es das war.

42.7 So Piglet put the jar at the bottom of the Pit, and
climbed out, and they went off home together.
Also stellte Ferkel den Krug auf den Boden der Grube,
kletterte hinaus und ging mit ihm nach Hause.

44.1 "Well, good night, Pooh," said Piglet,
"Gute Nacht, Puuh," sagte Ferkel,

44.2 when they had got to Pooh's house.
als sie in Puuhs Haus angekommen waren.

"And we meet at six o'clock to-morrow morning by
the Pine Trees, and see how many Heffalumps we've
got in our Trap." 44.3

"Und wir treffen uns morgen früh um sechs Uhr bei den
Kiefern, um zu sehen, wie viele Heffalumps wir in unserer
Falle haben."

"Six o'clock, Piglet. And have you got any string?" 45.1

"Sechs Uhr, Ferkel. Und hast du eine Schnur?"

"No. Why do you want string?" 46.1

"Nein. Warum willst du eine Schnur?"

"To lead them home with." 47.1

"Um sie damit nach Hause zu führen."

"Oh! ...I think Heffalumps come if you whistle." 48.1

"Oh! ...Ich glaube, Heffalumps kommen, wenn man pfeift."

"Some do and some don't. 49.1

"Manche tun es, manche nicht.

You never can tell with Heffalumps. Well, good
night!" 49.2

Bei Heffalumps kann man das nie wissen. Also, gute
Nacht!"

"Good night!" 50.1

"Gute Nacht!"

And off Piglet trotted to his house TRESPASSERS W, 51.1

Und Ferkel trottete zu seinem Haus TRESPASSERS W,

51.2 while Pooh made his preparations for bed.
während Puuh sich fürs Bett fertig machte.

52.1 Some hours later, just as the night was beginning to steal away, Pooh woke up suddenly with a sinking feeling.
Einige Stunden später, als die Nacht sich langsam davonschlich, wachte Puuh plötzlich mit einem mulmigen Gefühl auf.

52.2 He had had that sinking feeling before, and he knew what it meant.
Er hatte dieses Gefühl schon einmal gehabt, und er wusste, was es bedeutete.

52.3 He was hungry.
Er war hungrig.

52.4 So he went to the larder, and he stood on a chair and reached up to the top shelf, and found -
Also ging er zur Vorratskammer, stellte sich auf einen Stuhl und griff nach dem obersten Regal -

52.5 nothing.
und fand nichts.

53.1 "That's funny," he thought.
"Das ist komisch," dachte er.

53.2 "I know I had a jar of honey there.
"Ich weiß, dass ich dort ein Glas Honig hatte.

53.3 A full jar, full of honey right up to the top, and it had HUNNY written on it, so that I should know it was honey.
Ein volles Glas, bis oben hin voll mit Honig, und es stand HUNNY drauf, damit ich weiß, dass es Honig ist.

That's very funny."   53.4
Das ist sehr lustig."

And then he began to wander up and down,   53.5
wondering where it was and murmuring a murmur
to himself.
Und dann fing er an, auf und ab zu gehen, fragte sich, wo es
war und murmelte etwas vor sich hin.

Like this: 53.6
Etwa so:

It's very, very funny,   54.1
Das ist sehr, sehr lustig,

'Cos I   55.1
Denn ich

know   56.1
wissen

I had some honey;   57.1
Ich hatte etwas Honig;

'Cos it had a label on,   58.1
Weil es ein Etikett trug,

Saying HUNNY.   59.1
Ich sage HUNNY.

A goloptious full-up pot too,   60.1
Und ein prall gefüllter Topf,

61.1 **And I don't know where it's got to,**
Und ich weiß nicht, wo es geblieben ist,

62.1 **No, I don't know where it's gone — .**
Nein, ich weiß nicht, wo es hin ist.

63.1 **Well, it's funny.**
Nun, das ist schon komisch.

64.1 **He had murmured this to himself three times in a singing sort of way,**
Er hatte dies dreimal singend vor sich hingemurmelt,

64.2 **when suddenly he remembered.**
als er sich plötzlich erinnerte.

64.3 **He had put it into the Cunning Trap to catch the Heffalump.**
Er hatte ihn in die Gerissenenfalle gelegt, um den Heffalump zu fangen.

65.1 **"Bother!" said Pooh.**
"Ach was!" sagte Puuh.

65.2 **"It all comes of trying to be kind to Heffalumps."**
"Das kommt alles davon, wenn man versucht, nett zu Heffalumps zu sein."

65.3 **And he got back into bed.**
Und er ging zurück ins Bett.

66.1 **But he couldn't sleep.**
Aber er konnte nicht schlafen.

The more he tried to sleep, the more he couldn't. 66.2

Je mehr er versuchte zu schlafen, desto mehr konnte er
nicht.

He tried Counting Sheep, which is sometimes a good 66.3
way of getting to sleep, and, as that was no good, he
tried counting Heffalumps.

Er versuchte, Schafe zu zählen, was manchmal eine gute
Methode ist, um einzuschlafen, und als das nichts half,
versuchte er, Heffalumps zu zählen.

And that was worse. 66.4

Und das war noch schlimmer.

Because every Heffalump that he counted was 66.5
making straight for a pot of Pooh's honey, and eating
it all.

Denn jeder Heffalump, den er zählte, machte sich direkt
auf den Weg zu einem Topf mit Puuhs Honig und fraß ihn
auf.

For some minutes he lay there miserably, but when 66.6
the five hundred and eighty-seventh Heffalump was
licking its jaws, and saying to itself,

Einige Minuten lang lag er jämmerlich da, aber als der
fünfhundertsiebenundachtzigste Heffalump sich die
Kinnlade leckte und zu sich selbst sagte,

"Very good honey this, I don't know when I've tasted 66.7
better,"

"Das ist ein sehr guter Honig, ich weiß nicht, wann ich
jemals einen besseren gekostet habe,"

Pooh could bear it no longer. 66.8

konnte Puuh es nicht länger ertragen.

66.9 He jumped out of bed, he ran out of the house, and he ran straight to the Six Pine Trees.

Er sprang aus dem Bett, rannte aus dem Haus und lief geradewegs zu den Sechs Tannenbäumen.

68.1 The Sun was still in bed, but there was a lightness in the sky over the Hundred Acre Wood which seemed to show that it was waking up and would soon be kicking off the clothes.

Die Sonne lag noch im Bett, aber der Himmel über dem Hundertmorgenwald war so hell, dass man meinen konnte, sie sei aufgewacht und würde bald die Kleider ablegen.

68.2 In the half-light the Pine Trees looked cold and lonely, and the Very Deep Pit seemed deeper than it was, and Pooh's jar of honey at the bottom was something mysterious, a shape and no more.

Im Halbdunkel sahen die Kiefern kalt und einsam aus, und die sehr tiefe Grube schien tiefer zu sein, als sie war, und Puuhs Honigglas am Boden war etwas Geheimnisvolles, eine Gestalt und nicht mehr.

But as he got nearer to it his nose told him that it was
indeed honey, and his tongue came out and began to
polish up his mouth, ready for it.

68.3

Doch als er näher kam, verriet ihm seine Nase, dass es
sich tatsächlich um Honig handelte, und seine Zunge fuhr
heraus und begann, seinen Mund zu polieren, bereit für
den Honig.

"Bother!" said Pooh, as he got his nose inside the jar.

70.1

"Mist!" sagte Puuh, als er seine Nase in das Glas steckte.

"A Heffalump has been eating it!"

70.2

"Ein Heffalump hat es gegessen!"

And then he thought a little and said,

70.3

Dann dachte er kurz nach und sagte,

"Oh, no, I did. I forgot."

70.4

"Oh, nein, ich habe es gegessen. Ich habe es vergessen."

Indeed, he had eaten most of it.

71.1

Tatsächlich hatte er das meiste davon gegessen.

71.2 But there was a little left at the very bottom of the jar, and he pushed his head right in, and began to lick ...

Aber ganz unten im Glas war noch ein wenig übrig, und er steckte seinen Kopf hinein und begann zu lecken ...

73.1 By and by Piglet woke up.

Nach und nach wachte Ferkel auf.

73.2 As soon as he woke he said to himself, "Oh!"

Kaum war es aufgewacht, sagte es zu sich selbst, "Oh!"

73.3 Then he said bravely, "Yes," and then, still more bravely,

Dann sagte es tapfer, "Ja," und dann, noch tapferer,

73.4 "Quite so."

"Ganz recht."

73.5 But he didn't feel very brave, for the word which was really jiggeting about in his brain was

Aber es fühlte sich nicht sehr tapfer, denn das Wort, das in seinem Kopf herumspukte, war

73.6 "Heffalumps."

"Heffalumps."

What was a Heffalump like? 74.1
Wie war ein Heffalump?

Was it Fierce? 75.1
War es Fierce?

Did it come when you whistled? And how did it come? 76.1
Kam es, als du gepfiffen hast? Und wie ist es gekommen?

Was it Fond of Pigs at all? 77.1
War es überhaupt Fond of Pigs?

If it was Fond of Pigs, did it make any difference what sort of Pig? 78.1
Wenn es sich um "Fond of Pigs" handelte, machte es dann einen Unterschied, um welche Art von Schwein es sich handelte?

Supposing it was Fierce with Pigs, would it make any difference if the Pig had a grandfather called TRESPASSERS WILLIAM? 79.1
Angenommen, es war Fierce with Pigs, würde es einen Unterschied machen, wenn das Schwein einen Großvater namens TRESPASSERS WILLIAM hätte?

81.1 He didn't know the answer to any of these questions ...

Er wusste auf keine dieser Fragen eine Antwort ...

81.2 and he was going to see his first Heffalump in about an hour from now!

und in etwa einer Stunde würde er seinen ersten Heffalump sehen!

82.1 Of course Pooh would be with him,

Natürlich würde Pooh bei ihm sein,

82.2 and it was much more Friendly with two.

und zu zweit war es viel freundlicher.

82.3 But suppose Heffalumps were Very Fierce with Pigs and Bears?

Aber was, wenn Heffalumps mit Schweinen und Bären sehr böse wären?

Wouldn't it be better to pretend that he had a
headache, and couldn't go up to the Six Pine Trees
this morning?

82.4

Wäre es nicht besser, so zu tun, als ob er Kopfschmerzen
hätte und heute Morgen nicht zu den Sechs Tannen
hinaufgehen könnte?

But then suppose that it was a very fine day, and there
was no Heffalump in the trap, here he would be, in
bed all the morning, simply wasting his time for
nothing.

82.5

Aber angenommen, es war ein sehr schöner Tag und es war
kein Heffalump in der Falle, dann würde er den ganzen
Morgen im Bett liegen und seine Zeit umsonst vergeuden.

What should he do?

82.6

Was sollte er dann tun?

And then he had a Clever Idea.

83.1

Und dann hatte er eine schlaue Idee.

He would go up very quietly to the Six Pine Trees
now, peep very cautiously into the Trap, and see if
there was a Heffalump there.

83.2

Er würde jetzt ganz leise zu den sechs Kiefern hinaufgehen,
ganz vorsichtig in die Falle spähen und nachsehen, ob es
dort einen Heffalump gab.

And if there was, he would go back to bed, and if
there wasn't, he wouldn't.

83.3

Und wenn ja, würde er wieder ins Bett gehen, und wenn
nicht, dann eben nicht.

So off he went.

84.1

Also ging er los.

84.2 At first he thought that there wouldn't be a Heffalump in the Trap, and then he thought that there would, and as he got nearer he was sure that there would, because he could hear it heffalumping about it like anything.

Zuerst dachte er, es gäbe keinen Heffalump in der Falle, dann dachte er, es gäbe einen, und als er näher kam, war er sich sicher, es gäbe einen, denn er hörte, wie der Heffalump in der Falle herumhüpfte.

85.1 "Oh, dear, oh, dear, oh, dear!" said Piglet to himself.

"Oje, oje, oje, oje!" sagte Ferkel zu sich selbst.

85.2 And he wanted to run away.

Und es wollte weglaufen.

85.3 But somehow, having got so near, he felt that he must just see what a Heffalump was like.

Aber irgendwie hatte es das Gefühl, dass es einfach sehen musste, wie ein Heffalump aussah, nachdem es so nahe herangekommen war.

85.4 So he crept to the side of the Trap and looked in ...

Also kroch es an die Seite der Falle und schaute in ...

And all the time Winnie-the-Pooh had been trying to get the honey-jar off his head. 87.1

Und die ganze Zeit über hatte Winnie-the-Pooh versucht, das Honigglas von seinem Kopf zu bekommen.

The more he shook it, the more tightly it stuck. 87.2

Je mehr er ihn schüttelte, desto fester saß er fest.

"Bother!" he said, inside the jar, and "Oh, help!" 88.1

"Mist!" sagte er im Inneren des Gefäßes, und "Oh, Hilfe!"

and, mostly, "Ow!" 88.2

und vor allem "Au!"

And he tried bumping it against things, but as he couldn't see what he was bumping it against, it didn't help him; 88.3

Und er versuchte, es gegen Dinge zu stoßen, aber da er nicht sehen konnte, wogegen er es stieß, half ihm das nicht;

and he tried to climb out of the Trap, but as he could see nothing but jar, and not much of that, he couldn't find his way. 88.4

und er versuchte, aus der Falle herauszuklettern, aber da er nichts außer dem Glas sehen konnte, und davon nicht viel, konnte er den Weg nicht finden.

So at last he lifted up his head, jar and all, and made a loud, roaring noise of Sadness and Despair ... 88.5

Schließlich hob er seinen Kopf, mitsamt dem Glas, und stieß einen lauten, brüllenden Schrei der Traurigkeit und Verzweiflung aus ...

and it was at that moment that Piglet looked down. 88.6

und in diesem Moment sah Ferkel nach unten.

90.1 "Help, help!" cried Piglet, "a Heffalump,
"Hilfe, Hilfe!" rief Ferkel, "ein Heffalump,

90.2 a Horrible Heffalump!"
ein schrecklicher Heffalump!"

90.3 and he scampered off as hard as he could, still crying out,
und es huschte davon, so schnell es konnte, immer noch schreiend,

90.4 "Help, help, a Herrible Hoffalump!
"Hilfe, Hilfe, ein schrecklicher Hoffalump!

90.5 Hoff, Hoff, a Hellible Horralump!
Hoff, Hoff, ein Höllischer Horralump!

90.6 Holl, Holl, a Hoffable Hellerump!"
Holl, Holl, ein Hoffable Hellerump!"

90.7 And he didn't stop crying and scampering until he got to Christopher Robin's house.
Und er hörte nicht auf zu weinen und zu hüpfen, bis er bei Christopher Robins Haus ankam.

"Whatever's the matter, Piglet?" said Christopher Robin,

"Was ist denn los, Ferkel?" fragte Christopher Robin,

91.1

who was just getting up.

der gerade aufgestanden war.

91.2

"Heff,"

"Heff,"

92.1

said Piglet, breathing so hard that he could hardly speak,

sagte Ferkel und atmete so schwer, dass es kaum sprechen konnte,

92.2

"a Heff — a Heff — a Heffalump."

"ein Heff — a Heff — a Heffalump."

92.3

"Where?"

"Wo?"

93.1

"Up there," said Piglet, waving his paw.

"Da oben," sagte Ferkel und winkte mit der Pfote.

94.1

"What did it look like?"

"Wie hat es ausgesehen?"

95.1

"Like — like —— It had the biggest head you ever saw, Christopher Robin.

"Es hatte den größten Kopf, den du je gesehen hast, Christopher Robin.

96.1

A great enormous thing, like — like nothing.

Ein großes, riesiges Ding, wie ein Nichts.

96.2

96.3 **A huge big — well, like a — I don't know — like an enormous big nothing.**
Ein riesiges großes ...Na ja, wie ein ...Ich weiß nicht, wie ein riesiges großes Nichts.

96.4 **Like a jar."**
Wie ein Krug."

97.1 **"Well," said Christopher Robin, putting on his shoes,**
"Nun," sagte Christopher Robin und zog seine Schuhe an,

97.2 **"I shall go and look at it. Come on."**
"ich werde es mir ansehen. Komm mit."

99.1 **Piglet wasn't afraid if he had Christopher Robin with him, so off they went ...**
Ferkel hatte keine Angst, wenn er Christopher Robin bei sich hatte, und so gingen sie los ...

100.1 **"I can hear it, can't you?" said Piglet anxiously,**
"Ich kann es hören, du nicht?" sagte Ferkel ängstlich,

100.2 **as they got near.**
als sie näher kamen.

"I can hear something," said Christopher Robin.   101.1
"Ich kann etwas hören," sagte Christopher Robin.

It was Pooh bumping his head against a tree-root he   102.1
had found.
Es war Puuh, der mit dem Kopf gegen eine Wurzel stieß, die
er gefunden hatte.

"There!" said Piglet. "Isn't it awful?"   103.1
"Da!" sagte Ferkel. "Ist das nicht furchtbar?"

And he held on tight to Christopher Robin's hand.   103.2
Und er hielt sich an Christopher Robins Hand fest.

Suddenly Christopher Robin began to laugh ...   104.1
Plötzlich begann Christopher Robin zu lachen ...

and he laughed ...and he laughed ...and he laughed.   104.2
und er lachte ...und er lachte ...und er lachte.

And while he was still laughing -   104.3
Und während er noch lachte -

Crash went the Heffalump's head against the tree-   104.4
root, Smash went the jar, and out came Pooh's head
again ...
krachte der Kopf des Heffalump gegen die Baumwurzel,
krachte das Glas, und Poohs Kopf kam wieder heraus ...

126

106.1 Then Piglet saw what a Foolish Piglet he had been, and he was so ashamed of himself that he ran straight off home and went to bed with a headache.

Da sah Ferkel, was für ein dummes Ferkel es gewesen war, und es schämte sich so sehr, dass es sofort nach Hause lief und sich mit Kopfschmerzen ins Bett legte.

106.2 But Christopher Robin and Pooh went home to breakfast together.

Aber Christopher Robin und Puuh gingen nach Hause und frühstückten zusammen.

107.1 "Oh, Bear!" said Christopher Robin.

"Oh, Bär!" sagte Christopher Robin.

107.2 "How I do love you!"

"Wie sehr ich dich doch liebe!"

108.1 "So do I," said Pooh.

"Ich auch," sagte Pooh.

CHAPTER VI · IN WHICH EEYORE HAS A BIRTHDAY AND GETS TWO PRESENTS

KAPITEL VI · IN DEM EEYORE GEBURTSTAG HAT UND ZWEI GESCHENKE BEKOMMT

1.1 Eeyore, the old grey Donkey, stood by the side of the stream, and looked at himself in the water.

Eeyore, der alte graue Esel, stand am Ufer des Baches und betrachtete sich selbst im Wasser.

2.1 "Pathetic," he said. "That's what it is.

"Erbärmlich," sagte er. "Das ist es, was es ist.

2.2 Pathetic."

Erbärmlich."

3.1 He turned and walked slowly down the stream for twenty yards, splashed across it, and walked slowly back on the other side.

Er drehte sich um und ging langsam zwanzig Meter den Bach hinunter, plätscherte hinüber und ging auf der anderen Seite langsam zurück.

Then he looked at himself in the water again.   3.2

Dann betrachtete er sich wieder im Wasser.

"As I thought," he said.   4.1

"Wie ich dachte," sagte er.

"No better from this side.   4.2

"Von dieser Seite ist es nicht besser.

But nobody minds. Nobody cares. Pathetic,   4.3

Aber das stört niemanden. Niemanden kümmert es.
Erbärmlich,

that's what it is."   4.4

das ist es."

There was a crackling noise in the bracken behind   6.1
him,

Hinter ihm knisterte es im Gestrüpp,

6.2 **and out came Pooh.**
und Puuh kam heraus.

7.1 **"Good morning, Eeyore," said Pooh.**
"Guten Morgen, I-Aah," sagte Puuh.

8.1 **"Good morning, Pooh Bear," said Eeyore gloomily.**
"Guten Morgen, Puuh-Bär," sagte I-Aah düster.

8.2 **"If it is a good morning," he said.**
"Wenn es ein guter Morgen ist," sagte er.

8.3 **"Which I doubt," said he.**
"Was ich bezweifle," sagte er.

9.1 **"Why, what's the matter?"**
"Warum, was ist denn los?"

10.1 **"Nothing, Pooh Bear, nothing. We can't all,**
"Nichts, Puuh-Bär, nichts. Wir können nicht alle,

10.2 **and some of us don't.**
und einige von uns wollen nicht.

10.3 **That's all there is to it."**
Das ist alles, was es zu sagen gibt."

11.1 **"Can't all what?" said Pooh, rubbing his nose.**
"Können nicht alle was?" sagte Pooh und rieb sich die Nase.

12.1 **"Gaiety. Song-and-dance.**
"Fröhlichkeit. Singen und Tanzen.

Here we go round the mulberry bush." 12.2
Hier geht's um den Maulbeerstrauch."

"Oh!" said Pooh. He thought for a long time, and then asked, 13.1
"Oh!" sagte Puuh. Er dachte lange nach und fragte dann,

"What mulberry bush is that?" 13.2
"Was für ein Maulbeerstrauch ist das?"

"Bon-hommy," went on Eeyore gloomily. 14.1
"Bon-hommy," fuhr Eeyore düster fort.

"French word meaning bonhommy," he explained. 14.2
"Das ist das französische Wort für bonhommy," erklärte er.

"I'm not complaining, but There It Is." 14.3
"Ich will mich nicht beschweren, aber so ist es."

Pooh sat down on a large stone, 16.1
Puuh setzte sich auf einen großen Stein und versuchte,

and tried to think this out. 16.2
darüber nachzudenken.

16.3 It sounded to him like a riddle, and he was never much good at riddles, being a Bear of Very Little Brain.

Es hörte sich für ihn wie ein Rätsel an, und er war nie gut in Rätseln, da er ein Bär mit sehr wenig Hirn war.

16.4 So he sang Cottleston Pie instead:

Also sang er stattdessen Cottleston Pie:

17.1 Cottleston, Cottleston, Cottleston Pie,

Cottleston, Cottleston, Cottleston Pie,

18.1 A fly can't bird, but a bird can fly.

Eine Fliege kann nicht vögeln, aber ein Vogel kann fliegen.

19.1 Ask me a riddle and I reply:

Stell mir ein Rätsel und ich antworte:

20.1 "Cottleston, Cottleston, Cottleston Pie."

"Cottleston, Cottleston, Cottleston Pie."

21.1 That was the first verse.

Das war die erste Strophe.

21.2 When he had finished it, Eeyore didn't actually say that he didn't like it, so Pooh very kindly sang the second verse to him:

Als er fertig war, sagte I-Aah nicht wirklich, dass sie ihm nicht gefiel, also sang Puuh ihm freundlicherweise die zweite Strophe vor:

22.1 Cottleston, Cottleston, Cottleston Pie,

Cottleston, Cottleston, Cottleston Pie,

A fish can't whistle and neither can I. 23.1

Ein Fisch kann nicht pfeifen, und ich kann es auch nicht.

Ask me a riddle and I reply: 24.1

Stell mir ein Rätsel und ich antworte:

"Cottleston, Cottleston, Cottleston Pie." 25.1

"Cottleston, Cottleston, Cottleston Pie."

Eeyore still said nothing at all, 26.1

Eeyore sagte immer noch nichts,

so Pooh hummed the third verse quietly to himself: 26.2

und so summte Puuh die dritte Strophe leise vor sich hin:

Cottleston, Cottleston, Cottleston Pie, 27.1

Cottleston, Cottleston, Cottleston Pie,

Why does a chicken, I don't know why. 28.1

Ich weiß nicht, warum ein Huhn das tut.

Ask me a riddle and I reply: 29.1

Stell mir ein Rätsel und ich antworte:

"Cottleston, Cottleston, Cottleston Pie." 30.1

"Cottleston, Cottleston, Cottleston Pie."

32.1 "That's right," said Eeyore. "Sing. Umty-tiddly,
"Das stimmt," sagte I-Aah. "Sing. Umty-tiddly,

32.2 umty-too. Here we go gathering Nuts and May.
umty-too. Los geht's, wir sammeln Nüsse und Mai.

32.3 Enjoy yourself."
Amüsiert euch."

33.1 "I am," said Pooh.
"Das bin ich," sagte Puuh.

34.1 "Some can," said Eeyore.
"Manche können das," sagte I-Aah.

35.1 "Why, what's the matter?"
"Warum, was ist denn los?"

36.1 "Is anything the matter?"
"Stimmt etwas nicht?"

37.1 "You seem so sad, Eeyore."
"Du siehst so traurig aus, I- Aah."

"Sad? Why should I be sad? 38.1

"Traurig? Warum sollte ich traurig sein?

It's my birthday. The happiest day of the year." 38.2

Heute ist mein Geburtstag. Der schönste Tag des Jahres."

"Your birthday?" said Pooh in great surprise. 39.1

"Dein Geburtstag?" sagte Puuh sehr überrascht.

"Of course it is. Can't you see? 40.1

"Natürlich ist es das. Siehst du das nicht?

Look at all the presents I have had." 40.2

Sieh dir all die Geschenke an, die ich bekommen habe."

He waved a foot from side to side. 40.3

Er winkte mit einem Fuß hin und her.

"Look at the birthday cake. Candles and pink sugar." 40.4

"Sieh dir den Geburtstagskuchen an. Kerzen und rosa
Zucker."

Pooh looked — first to the right and then to the left. 41.1

Pooh schaute erst nach rechts und dann nach links.

"Presents?" said Pooh. "Birthday cake?" said Pooh. 42.1

"Geschenke?" sagte Puuh. "Geburtstagskuchen?" sagte
Puuh.

"Where?" 42.2

"Wo?"

"Can't you see them?" 43.1

"Kannst du sie nicht sehen?"

44.1 **"No," said Pooh.**
"Nein," sagte Puuh.

45.1 **"Neither can I," said Eeyore. "Joke,"**
"Das kann ich auch nicht," sagte I-Aah. "Ein Scherz,"

45.2 **he explained. "Ha ha!"**
erklärte er. "Ha ha!"

46.1 **Pooh scratched his head, being a little puzzled by all
this.**
Puuh kratzte sich am Kopf und war etwas verwirrt von all
dem.

47.1 **"But is it really your birthday?" he asked.**
"Aber hast du wirklich Geburtstag?" fragte er.

48.1 **"It is."**
"Das ist es."

49.1 **"Oh! Well, Many happy returns of the day, Eeyore."**
"Oh! Nun, ich wünsche dir einen schönen Tag, I- Aah."

50.1 **"And many happy returns to you, Pooh Bear."**
"Und alles Gute für dich, Puuh- Bär."

51.1 **"But it isn't my birthday."**
"Aber ich habe nicht Geburtstag."

52.1 **"No, it's mine."**
"Nein, es ist meins."

"But you said 'Many happy returns' —— "

53.1

"Aber Sie sagten 'Herzlichen Glückwunsch' ..."

"Well, why not?

54.1

"Nun, warum nicht?

You don't always want to be miserable on my
birthday,

54.2

Du willst doch nicht immer an meinem Geburtstag
unglücklich sein,

do you?"

54.3

oder?"

"Oh, I see," said Pooh.

55.1

"Oh, ich verstehe," sagte Puuh.

"It's bad enough,"

56.1

"Es ist schon schlimm genug,"

said Eeyore, almost breaking down,

56.2

sagte Eeyore und brach fast zusammen,

"being miserable myself, what with no presents
and no cake and no candles, and no proper notice
taken of me at all, but if everybody else is going to be
miserable too —— "

56.3

"selbst unglücklich zu sein, ohne Geschenke, ohne Kuchen,
ohne Kerzen und ohne dass man sich überhaupt um mich
kümmert, aber wenn alle anderen auch unglücklich sein
werden ..."

This was too much for Pooh. "Stay there!"

57.1

Das war zu viel für Puuh. "Bleib da!"

138

57.2 he called to Eeyore,

rief er I-Aah zu,

57.3 as he turned and hurried back home as quick as he could;

drehte sich um und eilte so schnell er konnte nach Hause;

57.4 for he felt that he must get poor Eeyore a present of some sort at once, and he could always think of a proper one afterwards.

denn er hatte das Gefühl, dass er dem armen I-Aah sofort ein Geschenk besorgen musste, und er konnte sich später immer noch ein passendes überlegen.

59.1 Outside his house he found Piglet, jumping up and down trying to reach the knocker.

Vor seinem Haus fand er Ferkel, das auf und ab sprang und versuchte, den Türklopfer zu erreichen.

60.1 "Hallo, Piglet," he said.

"Hallo, Ferkel," sagte er.

61.1 "Hallo, Pooh," said Piglet.

"Hallo, Puuh," sagte Ferkel.

"What are you trying to do?"   62.1

"Was haben Sie vor?"

"I was trying to reach the knocker," said Piglet.   63.1

"Ich habe versucht, den Klopfer zu erreichen," sagte Ferkel.

"I just came round —— "   63.2

"Ich kam gerade herum ..."

"Let me do it for you," said Pooh kindly.   64.1

"Lass mich das für dich tun," sagte Pooh freundlich.

So he reached up and knocked at the door.   64.2

Er ging hinauf und klopfte an die Tür.

"I have just seen Eeyore," he began,   64.3

"Ich habe gerade I-Aah gesehen," begann er,

"and poor Eeyore is in a Very Sad Condition, because   64.4
it's his birthday, and nobody has taken any notice of
it, and he's very Gloomy — you know what Eeyore
is — and there he was, and —— What a long time
whoever lives here is answering this door."

"und der arme I-Aah ist in einem sehr traurigen Zustand,
denn er hat Geburtstag, und niemand hat etwas davon
mitbekommen, und er ist sehr trübsinnig - ihr wisst ja, wie
I-Aah ist - und da war er, und - was für eine lange Zeit, wer
auch immer hier wohnt, macht diese Tür auf."

And he knocked again.   64.5

Und er klopfte erneut.

"But Pooh," said Piglet, "it's your own house!"   65.1

"Aber Puuh," sagte Ferkel, "es ist doch dein eigenes Haus!"

.

66.1 "Oh!" said Pooh. "So it is," he said. "Well,

"Oh!" sagte Puuh. "So ist es," sagte er. "Na,

66.2 let's go in."

dann lass uns reingehen."

67.1 So in they went.

Also gingen sie hinein.

67.2 The first thing Pooh did was to go to the cupboard
to see if he had quite a small jar of honey left; and he
had, so he took it down.

Als Erstes ging Puuh zum Schrank, um zu sehen, ob er noch
ein kleines Glas Honig übrig hatte, und das hatte er, also
nahm er es herunter.

69.1 "I'm giving this to Eeyore," he explained, "as a
present.

"Ich schenke das Eeyore," erklärte er, "als Geschenk.

69.2 What are you going to give?"

Was wirst du schenken?"

70.1 "Couldn't I give it too?" said Piglet.

"Könnte ich es nicht auch geben?" sagte Ferkel.

"From both of us?"   70.2
"Von uns beiden?"

"No," said Pooh. "That would not be a good plan."   71.1
"Nein," sagte Puuh. "Das wäre kein guter Plan."

"All right, then, I'll give him a balloon.   72.1
"Na gut, dann gebe ich ihm einen Luftballon.

I've got one left from my party.   72.2
Ich habe noch einen von meiner Party übrig.

I'll go and get it now, shall I?"   72.3
Ich werde ihn jetzt holen, ja?"

"That, Piglet, is a very good idea.   73.1
"Das, Ferkel, ist eine sehr gute Idee.

It is just what Eeyore wants to cheer him up.   73.2
Das ist genau das, was I-Aah braucht, um ihn aufzuheitern.

Nobody can be uncheered with a balloon."   73.3
Mit einem Luftballon kann man niemanden aufmuntern."

So off Piglet trotted; and in the other direction went   74.1
Pooh,
Ferkel trottete also los,

with his jar of honey.   74.2
und in die andere Richtung ging Puuh mit seinem
Honigglas.

142

76.1 **It was a warm day, and he had a long way to go.**
Es war ein warmer Tag, und er hatte einen langen Weg vor
sich.

76.2 **He hadn't gone more than half-way when a sort of
funny feeling began to creep all over him.**
Er hatte noch nicht einmal die Hälfte des Weges
zurückgelegt, als ihn ein seltsames Gefühl beschlich.

76.3 **It began at the tip of his nose and trickled all through
him and out at the soles of his feet.**
Es begann an seiner Nasenspitze und rieselte durch ihn
hindurch bis zu seinen Fußsohlen.

76.4 **It was just as if somebody inside him were saying,**
Es war, als ob jemand in ihm sagte,

76.5 **"Now then, Pooh, time for a little something."**
"So, Puuh, Zeit für eine Kleinigkeit."

77.1 **"Dear, dear," said Pooh,**
"Oje, oje," sagte Puuh,

77.2 **"I didn't know it was as late as that."**
"ich wusste nicht, dass es schon so spät ist."

So he sat down and took the top off his jar of honey.   77.3

Er setzte sich hin und nahm den Deckel seines
Honigglases ab.

"Lucky I brought this with me," he thought.   77.4

"Gut, dass ich das mitgebracht habe," dachte er.

"Many a bear going out on a warm day like this would   77.5
never have thought of bringing a little something
with him."

"Viele Bären, die an einem so warmen Tag unterwegs sind,
hätten nie daran gedacht, eine Kleinigkeit mitzunehmen."

And he began to eat.   77.6

Und er begann zu essen.

"Now let me see,"   79.1

"Mal sehen,"

he thought, as he took his last lick of the inside of the   79.2
jar,

dachte er, als er ein letztes Mal an der Innenseite des Glases
leckte,

79.3 "where was I going? Ah, yes, Eeyore." He got up
slowly.
"wo wollte ich hin? Ah, ja, I-Aah." Langsam erhob er sich.

80.1 And then, suddenly, he remembered.
Und dann erinnerte er sich plötzlich.

80.2 He had eaten Eeyore's birthday present!
Er hatte das Geburtstagsgeschenk von I-Aah gegessen!

81.1 "Bother!" said Pooh. "What shall I do?
"Mist!" sagte Puuh. "Was soll ich tun?

81.2 I must give him something."
Ich muss ihm etwas geben."

83.1 For a little while he couldn't think of anything.
Eine Zeit lang fiel ihm nichts ein.

83.2 Then he thought:
Dann dachte er,

"Well, it's a very nice pot, even if there's no honey in
it, and if I washed it clean, and got somebody to write

83.3

"Nun, es ist ein sehr schöner Topf, auch wenn kein Honig
drin ist, und wenn ich ihn sauber wasche und jemanden
dazu bringe

'A Happy Birthday'

83.4

'Alles Gute zum Geburtstag'

on it, Eeyore could keep things in it, which might be
Useful."

83.5

darauf zu schreiben, könnte Eeyore Dinge darin
aufbewahren, die vielleicht nützlich sind."

So, as he was just passing the Hundred Acre Wood, he
went inside to call on Owl, who lived there.

83.6

Als er gerade am Hundertmorgenwald vorbeikam, ging er
hinein, um Eule zu besuchen, die dort wohnte.

"Good morning, Owl," he said.

84.1

"Guten Morgen, Eule," sagte er.

"Good morning, Pooh," said Owl.

85.1

"Guten Morgen, Puuh," sagte Eule.

"Many happy returns of Eeyore's birthday," said
Pooh.

86.1

"Herzlichen Glückwunsch zu Eeyores Geburtstag," sagte
Puuh.

"Oh, is that what it is?"

87.1

"Ach, das ist es also?"

88.1 "What are you giving him, Owl?"
"Was gibst du ihm, Eule?"

89.1 "What are you giving him, Pooh?"
"Was gibst du ihm, Pooh?"

90.1 "I'm giving him a Useful Pot to Keep Things In,
"Ich schenke ihm einen nützlichen Topf zur Aufbewahrung,

90.2 and I wanted to ask you —— "
und ich wollte dich fragen ..."

91.1 "Is this it?" said Owl, taking it out of Pooh's paw.
"Ist es das?" sagte Eule und nahm es aus Puuhs Pfote.

92.1 "Yes, and I wanted to ask you —— "
"Ja, und ich wollte Sie fragen ..."

93.1 "Somebody has been keeping honey in it," said Owl.
"Jemand hat Honig darin aufbewahrt," sagte Eule.

94.1 "You can keep anything in it," said Pooh earnestly.
"Man kann alles darin aufbewahren," sagte Pooh ernsthaft.

94.2 "It's Very Useful like that. And I wanted to ask you —— "
"So ist es sehr nützlich. Und ich wollte dich fragen ..."

95.1 "You ought to write 'A Happy Birthday' on it."
"Du solltest 'A Happy Birthday' darauf schreiben."

147

"That was what I wanted to ask you," said Pooh.   96.1
"Genau das wollte ich dich fragen," sagte Pooh.

"Because my spelling is Wobbly.   96.2
"Denn meine Rechtschreibung ist wackelig.

It's good spelling but it Wobbles, and the letters get in   96.3
the wrong places.
Es ist eine gute Rechtschreibung, aber sie wackelt, und die
Buchstaben kommen an die falschen Stellen.

Would you write 'A Happy Birthday' on it for me?"   96.4
Könntest du 'Happy Birthday' für mich darauf schreiben?"

"It's a nice pot,"   97.1
"Das ist ein schöner Topf,"

said Owl, looking at it all round.   97.2
sagte Eule und betrachtete ihn von allen Seiten.

"Couldn't I give it too? From both of us?"   97.3
"Könnte ich ihn nicht auch schenken? Von uns beiden?"

"No," said Pooh. "That would not be a good plan.   98.1
"Nein," sagte Puuh. "Das wäre kein guter Plan.

Now I'll just wash it first,   98.2
Ich werde es erst waschen,

and then you can write on it."   98.3
und dann kannst du darauf schreiben."

99.1 Well, he washed the pot out, and dried it, while Owl
licked the end of his pencil, and wondered how to
spell

Nun, er wusch den Topf aus und trocknete ihn ab, während
Eule das Ende seines Bleistifts abschleckte und sich fragte,
wie man schreibt

99.2 "birthday."

"Geburtstag."

100.1 "Can you read, Pooh?" he asked a little anxiously.

"Kannst du lesen, Puuh?" fragte er ein wenig ängstlich.

100.2 "There's a notice about knocking and ringing outside
my door,

"Vor meiner Tür hängt ein Zettel über Klopfen und
Klingeln,

100.3 which Christopher Robin wrote. Could you read it?"

den Christopher Robin geschrieben hat. Kannst du ihn
lesen?"

101.1 "Christopher Robin told me what it said, and then I
could."

"Christopher Robin hat mir gesagt, was da steht, und dann
konnte ich es."

102.1 "Well, I'll tell you what this says, and then you'll be
able to."

"Nun, ich werde Ihnen sagen, was hier steht, und dann
werden Sie es können."

103.1 So Owl wrote ...and this is what he wrote:

Also schrieb Eule ...und das ist, was er schrieb:

HIPY PAPY BTHUTHDTH THUTHDA BTHUTHDY. 105.1
HIPY PAPY BTHUTHDTH THUTHDA BTHUTHDY.

Pooh looked on admiringly. 106.1
Puuh schaute bewundernd zu.

"I'm just saying 'A Happy Birthday'," said Owl 107.1
carelessly.
"Ich sage nur 'Alles Gute zum Geburtstag'," sagte Eule
achtlos.

"It's a nice long one," 108.1
"Es ist ein schönes, langes Stück,"

said Pooh, very much impressed by it. 108.2
sagte Puuh und war sehr beeindruckt davon.

"Well, actually, of course, I'm saying 109.1
"Nun, eigentlich sage ich natürlich

'A Very Happy Birthday with love from Pooh.' 109.2
'Alles Gute zum Geburtstag, mit Liebe von Pooh.'

109.3 Naturally it takes a good deal of pencil to say a long
thing like that."

Natürlich braucht man eine Menge Bleistift, um so etwas
Langes zu sagen."

110.1 "Oh, I see," said Pooh.

"Oh, ich verstehe," sagte Puuh.

111.1 While all this was happening, Piglet had gone back to
his own house to get Eeyore's balloon.

Während all dies geschah, war Ferkel in sein eigenes Haus
zurückgegangen, um I-Ahs Ballon zu holen.

111.2 He held it very tightly against himself, so that it
shouldn't blow away, and he ran as fast as he could so
as to get to Eeyore before Pooh did;

Er drückte ihn ganz fest an sich, damit er nicht wegflog,
und rannte so schnell er konnte, um vor Puuh bei I-Aah zu
sein;

111.3 for he thought that he would like to be the first one to
give a present, just as if he had thought of it without
being told by anybody.

denn er dachte, dass er gerne der Erste sein würde, der ein
Geschenk überreicht, so als ob er es sich ausgedacht hätte,
ohne dass es ihm jemand gesagt hätte.

111.4 And running along, and thinking how pleased Eeyore
would be, he didn't look where he was going …

Und während er rannte und dachte, wie sehr sich I-Aah
freuen würde, schaute er nicht, wohin er ging …

111.5 and suddenly he put his foot in a rabbit hole, and fell
down flat on his face.

und plötzlich trat er mit dem Fuß in ein Kaninchenloch
und fiel auf sein Gesicht.

BANG!? !? !? 113.1

BANG!? !? !?

Piglet lay there, wondering what had happened. 114.1

Ferkel lag da und fragte sich, was geschehen war.

At first he thought that the whole world had blown 114.2
up; and then he thought that perhaps only the Forest
part of it had; and then he thought that perhaps
only he had, and he was now alone in the moon or
somewhere, and would never see Christopher Robin
or Pooh or Eeyore again.

Zuerst dachte er, die ganze Welt sei in die Luft geflogen,
dann dachte er, vielleicht sei nur der Wald in die Luft
geflogen, und dann dachte er, vielleicht sei nur er in die
Luft geflogen, und er sei jetzt allein auf dem Mond oder
sonst wo und würde Christopher Robin oder Puuh oder
I-Aah nie wieder sehen.

And then he thought, 114.3

Und dann dachte er,

"Well, even if I'm in the moon, I needn't be face 114.4
downwards all the time,"

"Nun, selbst wenn ich im Mond bin, muss ich nicht die
ganze Zeit mit dem Gesicht nach unten sein,"

so he got cautiously up and looked about him. 114.5

und so stand er vorsichtig auf und sah sich um.

115.1 He was still in the Forest!
Er war immer noch im Wald!

116.1 "Well, that's funny," he thought.
"Nun, das ist komisch," dachte er.

116.2 "I wonder what that bang was.
"Ich frage mich, was dieser Knall war.

116.3 I couldn't have made such a noise just falling down.
So ein Geräusch kann ich doch nicht machen, wenn ich
einfach so hinfalle.

116.4 And where's my balloon?
Und wo ist mein Ballon?

116.5 And what's that small piece of damp rag doing?"
Und was macht dieses kleine Stück feuchten Lappens?"

117.1 It was the balloon!
Es war der Ballon!

118.1 "Oh, dear!" said Piglet
"Oh je!" sagte Ferkel

118.2 "Oh, dear, oh, dearie, dearie, dear! Well,
"oh je, oh je, oh je, oh je, oh je, oh je! Nun,

118.3 it's too late now.
jetzt ist es zu spät.

118.4 I can't go back, and I haven't another balloon, and
perhaps Eeyore doesn't like balloons so very much."
Ich kann nicht mehr zurück, und ich habe keinen Ballon
mehr, und vielleicht mag I-Aah keine Ballons so sehr."

So he trotted on, rather sadly now, and down he came   119.1
to the side of the stream where Eeyore was, and called
out to him.

So trabte er weiter, ziemlich traurig, und kam an das Ufer
des Baches, wo I-Aah war, und rief ihm zu.

"Good morning, Eeyore," shouted Piglet.   120.1

"Guten Morgen, I-Aah," rief Ferkel.

"Good morning, Little Piglet," said Eeyore.   121.1

"Guten Morgen, kleines Ferkel," sagte I-Aah.

"If it is a good morning," he said.   121.2

"Wenn es ein guter Morgen ist," sagte er.

"Which I doubt," said he. "Not that it matters,"   121.3

"Was ich bezweifle," sagte er. "Aber das macht nichts,"

he said.   121.4

sagte er.

"Many happy returns of the day," said Piglet,   122.1

"Ich wünsche dir alles Gute für den Tag," sagte Ferkel,

having now got closer.   122.2

das nun näher gekommen war.

Eeyore stopped looking at himself in the stream, and   123.1
turned to stare at Piglet.

I-Aah hörte auf, sich im Bach zu betrachten, und drehte
sich um, um Ferkel anzustarren.

"Just say that again," he said.   124.1

"Sagen Sie das noch einmal," sagte er.

125.1 "Many hap —— "
"Viele hap ..."

126.1 "Wait a moment."
"Warten Sie einen Moment."

127.1 Balancing on three legs, he began to bring his fourth
leg very cautiously up to his ear.
Auf drei Beinen balancierend, begann er, sein viertes Bein
ganz vorsichtig bis zu seinem Ohr zu führen.

127.2 "I did this yesterday," he explained,
"Das habe ich gestern gemacht," erklärte er,

127.3 as he fell down for the third time. "It's quite easy.
als er zum dritten Mal hinfiel. "Es ist ganz einfach.

127.4 It's so as I can hear better ...There, that's done it!
Es ist so, dass ich besser hören kann ...So, das war's!

127.5 Now then, what were you saying?"
Nun denn, was sagten Sie?"

127.6 He pushed his ear forward with his hoof.
Er schob sein Ohr mit dem Huf vor.

"Many happy returns of the day," said Piglet again. 129.1
"Ich wünsche dir einen schönen Tag," sagte Ferkel wieder.

"Meaning me?" 130.1
"Meinst du mich?"

"Of course, Eeyore." 131.1
"Natürlich, I- Aah."

"My birthday?" 132.1
"Mein Geburtstag?"

"Yes." 133.1
"Ja."

"Me having a real birthday?" 134.1
"Ich habe einen richtigen Geburtstag?"

"Yes, Eeyore, and I've brought you a present." 135.1
"Ja, I-Aah, und ich habe dir ein Geschenk mitgebracht."

Eeyore took down his right hoof from his right ear, 136.1
turned round, and with great difficulty put up his left
hoof.
Eeyore nahm seinen rechten Huf von seinem rechten Ohr
herunter, drehte sich um und setzte mühsam seinen linken
Huf auf.

"I must have that in the other ear," he said. 137.1
"Das muss ich auf dem anderen Ohr haben," sagte er.

"Now then." 137.2
"Nun denn."

138.1   "A present," said Piglet very loudly.
"Ein Geschenk," sagte Ferkel sehr laut.

139.1   "Meaning me again?"
"Meinst du wieder mich?"

140.1   "Yes."
"Ja."

141.1   "My birthday still?"
"Habe ich noch Geburtstag?"

142.1   "Of course, Eeyore."
"Natürlich, I- Aah."

143.1   "Me going on having a real birthday?"
"Ich soll einen richtigen Geburtstag feiern?"

144.1   "Yes, Eeyore, and I brought you a balloon."
"Ja, I-Aah, und ich habe dir einen Luftballon mitgebracht."

146.1   "Balloon?" said Eeyore. "You did say balloon?
"Ballon?" sagte I-Aah. "Du hast Luftballon gesagt?

One of those big coloured things you blow up? 146.2
Eins von diesen großen bunten Dingern, die man aufbläst?

Gaiety, song-and-dance, here we are and there we 146.3
are?"
Fröhlichkeit, Gesang und Tanz, hier sind wir und dort sind
wir?"

"Yes, but I'm afraid - I'm very sorry, Eeyore - 147.1
"Ja, aber ich fürchte - es tut mir sehr leid, I- Aah -

but when I was running along to bring it you, I fell 147.2
down."
aber als ich loslief, um es dir zu bringen, bin ich
hingefallen."

"Dear, dear, how unlucky! You ran too fast, 148.1
"Oje, oje, wie unglücklich! Du bist zu schnell gerannt,

I expect. You didn't hurt yourself, 148.2
nehme ich an. Du hast dich doch nicht verletzt,

Little Piglet?" 148.3
kleines Ferkel?"

"No, but I — I — oh, Eeyore, I burst the balloon!" 149.1
"Nein, aber ich ...oh, I-Aah, ich habe den Ballon platzen
lassen!"

There was a very long silence. 150.1
Es herrschte eine sehr lange Stille.

"My balloon?" said Eeyore at last. 151.1
"Mein Ballon?" sagte I-Aah schließlich.

158

152.1 **Piglet nodded.**
Ferkel nickte.

153.1 **"My birthday balloon?"**
"Mein Geburtstagsballon?"

154.1 **"Yes, Eeyore," said Piglet sniffing a little.**
"Ja, I-Aah," sagte Ferkel und schnüffelte ein wenig.

154.2 **"Here it is. With — with many happy returns of the day."**
"Hier ist es. Mit — mit vielen guten Wünschen für den Tag."

154.3 **And he gave Eeyore the small piece of damp rag.**
Und er gab I-Aah das kleine Stück feuchten Lappens.

155.1 **"Is this it?" said Eeyore, a little surprised.**
"Ist das alles?" fragte Eeyore ein wenig überrascht.

156.1 **Piglet nodded.**
Ferkel nickte.

157.1 **"My present?"**
"Mein Geschenk?"

158.1 **Piglet nodded again.**
Ferkel nickte wieder.

159.1 **"The balloon?"**
"Der Ballon?"

"Yes. "
160.1

"Ja. "

"Thank you, Piglet," said Eeyore.
161.1

"Danke, Ferkel," sagte I-Aah.

"You don't mind my asking," he went on,
161.2

"Wenn ich fragen darf," fuhr er fort,

"but what colour was this balloon when it — when it
161.3
was a balloon?"

"welche Farbe hatte dieser Ballon, als er ein Ballon war?"

"Red."
162.1

"Rot."

"I just wondered …Red," he murmured to himself.
163.1

"Ich habe mich nur gewundert …Rot," murmelte er vor
sich hin.

"My favourite colour …How big was it?"
163.2

"Meine Lieblingsfarbe …Wie groß war sie?"

"About as big as me. "
164.1

"Ungefähr so groß wie ich."

"I just wondered …About as big as Piglet,"
165.1

"Ich habe mich nur gewundert …Ungefähr so groß wie
Ferkel,"

he said to himself sadly. "My favourite size.
165.2

sagte er traurig zu sich selbst. "Meine Lieblingsgröße.

165.3 Well, well."

Sieh an, sieh an."

166.1 Piglet felt very miserable,

Ferkel fühlte sich sehr unglücklich und wusste nicht,

166.2 and didn't know what to say.

was es sagen sollte.

166.3 He was still opening his mouth to begin something,
and then deciding that it wasn't any good saying that,
when he heard a shout from the other side of the
river, and there was Pooh.

Er öffnete gerade den Mund, um etwas zu sagen, und
beschloss dann, dass es keinen Sinn hatte, das zu sagen,
als er einen Schrei von der anderen Seite des Flusses hörte,
und da war Puuh.

167.1 "Many happy returns of the day,"

"Ich wünsche dir einen schönen Tag,"

167.2 called out Pooh, forgetting that he had said it already.

rief Puuh und vergaß dabei, dass er es bereits gesagt hatte.

168.1 "Thank you, Pooh, I'm having them," said Eeyore
gloomily.

"Danke, Puuh, ich nehme sie," sagte I-Aah düster.

169.1 "I've brought you a little present,"

"Ich habe dir ein kleines Geschenk mitgebracht,"

169.2 said Pooh excitedly.

sagte Puuh aufgeregt.

"I've had it," said Eeyore. 170.1

"Ich habe die Nase voll," sagte Eeyore.

Pooh had now splashed across the stream to Eeyore, 171.1
and Piglet was sitting a little way off, his head in his
paws, snuffling to himself.

Puuh war inzwischen über den Bach zu I-Aah geplatscht,
und Ferkel saß etwas abseits, den Kopf in den Pfoten, und
schnüffelte vor sich hin.

"It's a Useful Pot," said Pooh. "Here it is. 172.1

"Es ist ein Nützlicher Topf," sagte Pooh. "Hier ist er.

And it's got 'A Very Happy Birthday with love from 172.2
Pooh'

Und es steht 'Alles Gute zum Geburtstag mit Liebe von
Pooh'

written on it. That's what all that writing is. 172.3

drauf. Das ist die ganze Schrift.

And it's for putting things in. There!" 172.4

Und da kann man Sachen rein tun. So!"

When Eeyore saw the pot, he became quite excited. 173.1

Als Eeyore den Topf sah, wurde er ganz aufgeregt.

"Why!" he said. 174.1

"Warum!" sagte er.

"I believe my Balloon will just go into that Pot!" 174.2

"Ich glaube, mein Ballon wird einfach in diesen Topf
fallen!"

162

175.1 "Oh, no, Eeyore," said Pooh.
"Oh, nein, I-Aah," sagte Puuh.

175.2 "Balloons are much too big to go into Pots.
"Ballons sind viel zu groß, um in Töpfe zu passen.

175.3 What you do with a balloon is, you hold the
ballon —— "
Was man mit einem Ballon macht, ist, dass man den Ballon
festhält ..."

176.1 "Not mine," said Eeyore proudly. "Look, Piglet!"
"Nicht meine," sagte I-Aah stolz. "Schau, Ferkel!"

176.2 And as Piglet looked sorrowfully round, Eeyore
picked the balloon up with his teeth, and placed it
carefully in the pot;
Und während Ferkel sich traurig umschaute, hob I-Aah den
Ballon mit seinen Zähnen auf und legte ihn vorsichtig in
den Topf;

176.3 picked it out and put it on the ground;
er nahm ihn heraus und legte ihn auf den Boden;

176.4 and then picked it up again and put it carefully back.
und dann hob er ihn wieder auf und legte ihn vorsichtig
zurück.

177.1 "So it does!" said Pooh. "It goes in!"
"So ist es!" sagte Puuh. "Es geht rein!"

178.1 "So it does!" said Piglet. "And it comes out!"
"So ist es!" sagte Ferkel. "Und es kommt heraus!"

"Doesn't it?" said Eeyore. 179.1
"Nicht wahr?" sagte I-Aah.

"It goes in and out like anything." 179.2
"Es geht rein und raus wie alles andere."

"I'm very glad," said Pooh happily, 180.1
"Ich bin sehr froh," sagte Pooh fröhlich,

"that I thought of giving you a Useful Pot to put 180.2
things in."
"dass ich daran gedacht habe, dir einen Nützlichen Topf zu
schenken, in den du deine Sachen tun kannst."

"I'm very glad," said Piglet happily, 181.1
"Ich bin sehr froh," sagte Ferkel fröhlich,

"that I thought of giving you Something to put in a 181.2
Useful Pot."
"dass ich daran gedacht habe, dir etwas zu geben, das du in
einen nützlichen Topf tun kannst."

But Eeyore wasn't listening. 182.1
Aber I-Aah hat nicht zugehört.

He was taking the balloon out, and putting it back 182.2
again, as happy as could be …
Er nahm den Ballon heraus und steckte ihn wieder hinein,
so glücklich, wie er nur sein konnte …

184.1   "And didn't I give him anything?"
"Und habe ich ihm nichts gegeben?"

184.2   asked Christopher Robin sadly.
fragte Christopher Robin traurig.

185.1   "Of course you did," I said.
"Natürlich hast du das," sagte ich.

185.2   "You gave him — don't you remember — a little — a little —— "
"Du hast ihm - erinnerst du dich nicht - ein bisschen - ein bisschen -"

186.1   "I gave him a box of paints to paint things with."
"Ich habe ihm eine Schachtel mit Farben gegeben, damit er etwas malen kann."

187.1   "That was it."
"Das war's."

188.1   "Why didn't I give it to him in the morning?"
"Warum habe ich es ihm nicht schon am Morgen gegeben?"

"You were so busy getting his party ready for him.   189.1

"Du warst so damit beschäftigt, seine Party für ihn
vorzubereiten.

He had a cake with icing on the top, and three   189.2
candles, and his name in pink sugar, and —— "

Er hatte einen Kuchen mit Zuckerguss und drei Kerzen und
seinen Namen in rosa Zucker und ..."

"Yes, I remember," said Christopher Robin.   190.1

"Ja, ich erinnere mich," sagte Christopher Robin.

CHAPTER VII · IN WHICH KANGA AND BABY ROO COME TO THE FOREST, AND PIGLET HAS A BATH

KAPITEL VII · IN DEM KANGA UND
BABY-ROO IN DEN WALD KOMMEN UND
DAS SCHWEINCHEN EIN BAD NIMMT

1.1 Nobody seemed to know where they came from, but there they were in the Forest:

Niemand schien zu wissen, woher sie kamen, aber da waren sie im Wald:

1.2 Kanga and Baby Roo. When Pooh asked Christopher Robin,

Kanga und Baby Ruh. Als Puuh Christopher Robin fragte,

1.3 "How did they come here?" Christopher Robin said,

"Wie sind sie hierher gekommen?" Christopher Robin sagte,

1.4 "In the Usual Way, if you know what I mean, Pooh,"

"Auf die übliche Weise, wenn du weißt, was ich meine, Puuh,"

and Pooh, who didn't, said "Oh!"   1.5
und Puuh, der das nicht wusste, sagte, "Oh!"

Then he nodded his head twice and said,   1.6
Dann nickte er zweimal mit dem Kopf und sagte,

"In the Usual Way. Ah!"   1.7
"Auf die übliche Art und Weise. Ah!"

Then he went to call upon his friend Piglet to see what   1.8
he thought about it.
Dann ging er zu seinem Freund Ferkel, um zu sehen, was er
darüber dachte.

And at Piglet's house he found Rabbit.   1.9
Und in Ferkels Haus fand er Kaninchen.

So they all talked about it together.   1.10
So sprachen sie alle zusammen darüber.

"What I don't like about it is this," said Rabbit.   3.1
"Was mir daran nicht gefällt, ist Folgendes," sagte Rabbit.

3.2 "Here are we — you, Pooh, and you, Piglet, and Me —
and suddenly —— "

"Da sind wir - du, Puuh, und du, Ferkel, und ich - und
plötzlich ..."

4.1 "And Eeyore," said Pooh.

"Und I-Aah," sagte Puuh.

5.1 "And Eeyore — and then suddenly —— "

"Und I-Aah - und dann plötzlich ..."

6.1 "And Owl," said Pooh.

"Und Eule," sagte Puuh.

7.1 "And Owl — and then all of a sudden —— "

"Und Eule - und dann ganz plötzlich ..."

8.1 "Oh, and Eeyore," said Pooh. "I was forgetting him."

"Oh, und I-Aah," sagte Puuh. "Ich habe ihn vergessen."

9.1 "Here — we — are," said Rabbit very slowly and
carefully,

"Hier sind wir," sagte der Hase ganz langsam und
vorsichtig,

9.2 "all — of — us, and then, suddenly, we wake up one
morning and, what do we find?

"wir alle, und dann wachen wir eines Morgens plötzlich auf
und was finden wir?

9.3 We find a Strange Animal among us.

Wir finden ein seltsames Tier unter uns.

An animal of whom we have never even heard before!   9.4
Ein Tier, von dem wir noch nie zuvor gehört haben!

An animal who carries her family about with her in   9.5
her pocket!
Ein Tier, das seine Familie in seiner Tasche mit sich
herumträgt!

Suppose I carried my family about with me in my   9.6
pocket, how many pockets should I want?"
Angenommen, ich würde meine Familie in meiner Tasche
mit mir herumtragen, wie viele Taschen bräuchte ich
dann?"

"Sixteen," said Piglet.   10.1
"Sechzehn," sagte Ferkel.

"Seventeen, isn't it?" said Rabbit.   11.1
"Siebzehn, nicht wahr?" sagte Rabbit.

"And one more for a handkerchief - that's eighteen.   11.2
"Und noch eine für ein Taschentuch - das macht achtzehn.

Eighteen pockets in one suit! I haven't time."   11.3
Achtzehn Taschen in einem Anzug! Ich habe keine Zeit."

There was a long and thoughtful silence ...   12.1
Es herrschte ein langes, nachdenkliches Schweigen ...

and then Pooh, who had been frowning very hard for   12.2
some minutes, said:
und dann sagte Puuh, der schon seit einigen Minuten die
Stirn sehr angestrengt gerunzelt hatte:

"I make it fifteen."   12.3
"Ich mache fünfzehn."

13.1 "What?" said Rabbit.

"Was?" sagte Kaninchen.

14.1 "Fifteen."

"Fünfzehn."

15.1 "Fifteen what?"

"Fünfzehn was?"

16.1 "Your family."

"Deine Familie."

17.1 "What about them?"

"Was ist mit ihnen?"

18.1 Pooh rubbed his nose and said that he thought Rabbit
had been talking about his family.

Puuh rieb sich die Nase und sagte, dass er dachte, Rabbit
hätte von seiner Familie gesprochen.

19.1 "Did I?" said Rabbit carelessly.

"Habe ich das?" sagte Kaninchen achtlos.

20.1 "Yes, you said —— "

"Ja, Sie sagten ..."

21.1 "Never mind, Pooh," said Piglet impatiently.

"Ist doch egal, Puuh," sagte Ferkel ungeduldig.

22.1 "The question is, What are we to do about Kanga?"

"Die Frage ist: Was machen wir mit Kanga?"

"Oh, I see," said Pooh.   23.1
"Oh, ich verstehe," sagte Puuh.

"The best way," said Rabbit, "would be this.   24.1
"Der beste Weg," sagte Rabbit, "wäre der folgende.

The best way would be to steal Baby Roo and hide   24.2
him, and then when Kanga says,
Am besten wäre es, Baby Ruh zu stehlen und zu verstecken,
und wenn Kanga dann fragt,

'Where's Baby Roo?' we say, 'Aha! "'   24.3
'Wo ist Baby Ruh?' sagen wir, 'Aha! "'

"Aha!" said Pooh, practising. "Aha! Aha! ...Of   25.1
course,"
"Aha!" sagte Puuh und übte. "Aha! Aha! ...Natürlich,"

he went on, "we could say 'Aha!'   25.2
fuhr er fort, "könnten wir 'Aha!'

even if we hadn't stolen Baby Roo."   25.3
auch dann sagen, wenn wir den kleinen Ruh nicht
gestohlen hätten."

"Pooh," said Rabbit kindly,   26.1
"Puuh," sagte Kaninchen freundlich,

"you haven't any brain."   26.2
"du hast keinen Verstand."

"I know," said Pooh humbly.   27.1
"Ich weiß," sagte Pooh bescheiden.

172

28.1 **"We say 'Aha!'**
"Wir sagen 'Aha!'

28.2 **so that Kanga knows that we know where Baby Roo is. 'Aha!'**
damit Kanga weiß, dass wir wissen, wo Baby Roo ist. 'Aha!'

28.3 **means**
bedeutet,

28.4 **'We'll tell you where Baby Roo is, if you promise to go away from the Forest and never come back.'**
'Wir sagen dir, wo Baby Ruh ist, wenn du versprichst, den Wald zu verlassen und nie wiederzukommen.'

28.5 **Now don't talk while I think."**
Und jetzt nicht reden, während ich nachdenke."

29.1 **Pooh went into a corner and tried saying 'Aha!'**
Puuh ging in eine Ecke und versuchte, mit dieser Stimme 'Aha!'

29.2 **in that sort of voice.**
zu sagen.

29.3 **Sometimes it seemed to him that it did mean what Rabbit said, and sometimes it seemed to him that it didn't.**
Manchmal schien es ihm, dass es das bedeutete, was Rabbit sagte, und manchmal schien es ihm, dass es das nicht tat.

29.4 **"I suppose it's just practice," he thought.**
"Ich nehme an, es ist nur Übung," dachte er.

"I wonder if Kanga will have to practise too so as to
understand it."

29.5

"Ich frage mich, ob Kanga auch üben muss, um es zu
verstehen."

"There's just one thing," said Piglet, fidgeting a bit.

30.1

"Da ist nur eine Sache," sagte Ferkel und zappelte ein
wenig.

"I was talking to Christopher Robin, and he said that
a Kanga was Generally Regarded as One of the Fiercer
Animals.

30.2

"Ich habe mich mit Christopher Robin unterhalten, und
er sagte, dass ein Kanga im Allgemeinen als eines der
wildesten Tiere angesehen wird.

I am not frightened of Fierce Animals in the ordinary
way, but it is well known that, if One of the Fiercer
Animals is Deprived of Its Young, it becomes as fierce
as Two of the Fiercer Animals.

30.3

Ich habe normalerweise keine Angst vor wilden Tieren,
aber es ist allgemein bekannt, dass ein wildes Tier, wenn
es seiner Jungen beraubt wird, so wild wird wie zwei wilde
Tiere.

In which case 'Aha!' is perhaps a foolish thing to say."

30.4

In diesem Fall 'Aha!' ist es vielleicht töricht zu sagen."

"Piglet,"

31.1

"Ferkel,"

said Rabbit, taking out a pencil, and
licking the end of it,

31.2

sagte der Hase, nahm einen Bleistift heraus und leckte an
dessen Ende,

174

31.3 "you haven't any pluck."
"du hast keinen Mut."

32.1 "It is hard to be brave,"
"Es ist schwer, mutig zu sein,"

32.2 said Piglet, sniffing slightly,
sagte Ferkel und schniefte leicht,

32.3 "when you're only a Very Small Animal."
"wenn man nur ein sehr kleines Tier ist."

34.1 Rabbit, who had begun to write very busily, looked
up and said:
Kaninchen, das sehr eifrig zu schreiben begonnen hatte,
blickte auf und sagte, "Das ist nicht wahr:

35.1 "It is because you are a very small animal that you
will be Useful in the adventure before us."
"Gerade weil du ein sehr kleines Tier bist, wirst du bei dem
vor uns liegenden Abenteuer nützlich sein."

Piglet was so excited at the idea of being Useful, 36.1
that he forgot to be frightened any more, and when
Rabbit went on to say that Kangas were only Fierce
during the winter months, being at other times of an
Affectionate Disposition, he could hardly sit still, he
was so eager to begin being useful at once.

Ferkel war von der Idee, nützlich zu sein, so begeistert,
dass es vergaß, sich zu fürchten, und als Kaninchen weiter
erzählte, dass Kangas nur in den Wintermonaten wild
seien, während sie zu anderen Zeiten eine liebevolle
Gesinnung hätten, konnte es kaum stillsitzen, so eifrig
war es, sich sofort nützlich zu machen.

"What about me?" said Pooh sadly. 37.1

"Was ist mit mir?" sagte Pooh traurig.

"I suppose I shan't be useful?" 37.2

"Ich nehme an, ich werde nicht von Nutzen sein?"

"Never mind, Pooh," said Piglet comfortingly. 38.1

"Mach dir nichts draus, Puuh," sagte Ferkel tröstend.

"Another time perhaps." 38.2

"Ein andermal vielleicht."

"Without Pooh," 39.1

"Ohne Pooh,"

said Rabbit solemnly as he sharpened his pencil, 39.2

sagte Rabbit feierlich, während er seinen Bleistift anspitzte,

"the adventure would be impossible." 39.3

"wäre das Abenteuer unmöglich."

40.1 "Oh!" said Piglet, and tried not to look disappointed.
"Oh," sagte Ferkel und versuchte, nicht enttäuscht
auszusehen.

40.2 But Pooh went into a corner of the room and said
proudly to himself,
Puuh aber ging in eine Ecke des Zimmers und sagte stolz zu
sich selbst,

40.3 "Impossible without Me! That sort of Bear."
"Unmöglich ohne mich! Diese Art von Bär."

41.1 "Now listen all of you,"
"Hört alle zu,"

41.2 said Rabbit when he had finished writing, and
Pooh and Piglet sat listening very eagerly with their
mouths open.
sagte Hase, als er mit dem Schreiben fertig war, und Puuh
und Ferkel saßen mit offenen Mündern da und hörten
gespannt zu.

41.3 This was what Rabbit read out:
Das war es, was Hase vorlas:

42.1 PLAN TO CAPTURE BABY ROO
PLAN ZUM EINFANGEN VON KÄNGURUBABYS

42.1

1.
1.

**General Remarks.
Kanga runs faster than
any of Us, even Me.**

Allgemeine
Bemerkungen. Kanga
läuft schneller als jeder
von uns, sogar ich.

2.
2.

**More General
Remarks. Kanga never
takes her eye off Baby
Roo, except when he's
safely buttoned up in
her pocket.**

Weitere allgemeine
Bemerkungen. Kanga
lässt Baby Roo nie aus
den Augen, außer wenn
er sicher in ihrer Tasche
verstaut ist.

3.

Therefore. If we are to capture Baby Roo, we must get a Long Start, because Kanga runs faster than any of Us, even Me. (See 1.)

3.

Deshalb. Wenn wir Baby Ruh fangen wollen, müssen wir einen langen Anlauf nehmen, denn Kanga läuft schneller als jeder von uns, sogar ich. (Siehe 1.)

4.

A Thought. If Roo had jumped out of Kanga's pocket and Piglet had jumped in, Kanga wouldn't know the difference, because Piglet is a Very Small Animal.

4.

Ein Gedanke. Wenn Ruh aus Kangas Tasche gesprungen wäre und Ferkel hineingesprungen wäre, würde Kanga den Unterschied nicht bemerken, weil Ferkel ein sehr kleines Tier ist.

5.

Like Roo.

5.

Wie Roo.

6.

But Kanga would have to be looking the other way first, so as not to see Piglet jumping in.

6.

Aber Kanga müsste zuerst in die andere Richtung schauen, damit er nicht sieht, wie Ferkel hineinspringt.

7.

See 2.

7.

Siehe 2.

8.

Another Thought. But if Pooh was talking to her very excitedly, she might look the other way for a moment.

8.

Ein anderer Gedanke. Aber wenn Pooh sehr aufgeregt mit ihr spricht, könnte sie für einen Moment wegschauen.

9.

And then I could run
away with Roo.

9. Und dann könnte ich mit
Roo weglaufen.

10.

Quickly.

10. Schnell.

11.

And Kanga wouldn't
discover the difference
until Afterwards.

11. Und Kanga würde den
Unterschied erst danach
entdecken.

55.1 Well, Rabbit read this out proudly, and for a little
while after he had read it nobody said anything.
Nun, Hase las dies stolz vor, und eine Weile sagte niemand
etwas, nachdem er es vorgelesen hatte.

And then Piglet, who had been opening and shutting
his mouth without making any noise, managed to say
very huskily:

55.2

Und dann schaffte es Ferkel, das seinen Mund auf - und
zugemacht hatte, ohne ein Geräusch zu machen, sehr leise
zu sagen:

"And — Afterwards?"

56.1

"Und danach?"

"How do you mean?"

57.1

"Wie meinen Sie das?"

"When Kanga does Discover the Difference?"

58.1

"Wann entdeckt Kanga den Unterschied?"

"Then we all say 'Aha! "'

59.1

"Dann sagen wir alle 'Aha! "'

"All three of us?"

60.1

"Wir alle drei?"

"Yes."

61.1

"Ja."

"Oh!"

62.1

"Oh!"

"Why, what's the trouble, Piglet?"

63.1

"Warum, was ist denn los, Ferkel?"

"Nothing," said Piglet, "as long as we all three say it.

64.1

"Nichts," sagte Ferkel, "solange wir es alle drei sagen.

64.2 As long as we all three say it," said Piglet,
Solange wir es alle drei sagen," sagte Ferkel,

64.3 "I don't mind," he said, "but I shouldn't care to say
"stört es mich nicht," sagte er, "aber ich würde

64.4 'Aha!' by myself.
'Aha!' nicht gerne allein sagen.

64.5 It wouldn't sound nearly so well. By the way," he said,
Es würde nicht annähernd so gut klingen. Übrigens,"
sagte er,

64.6 "you are quite sure about what you said about the
winter months?"
"bist du dir ganz sicher, was du über die Wintermonate
gesagt hast?"

65.1 "The winter months?"
"Die Wintermonate?"

66.1 "Yes, only being Fierce in the Winter Months."
"Ja, ich bin nur in den Wintermonaten heftig."

67.1 "Oh, yes, yes, that's all right. Well, Pooh?
"Oh, ja, ja, das ist in Ordnung. Nun, Puuh?

67.2 You see what you have to do?"
Siehst du, was du zu tun hast?"

68.1 "No," said Pooh Bear. "Not yet," he said.
"Nein," sagte Puuh-Bär. "Noch nicht," sagte er.

68.2 "What do I do?"
"Was soll ich tun?"

"Well, you just have to talk very hard to Kanga so as   69.1
she doesn't notice anything."
"Na ja, du musst nur ganz fest mit Kanga reden, damit sie
nichts merkt."

"Oh! What about?"   70.1
"Oh! Worüber?"

"Anything you like."   71.1
"Alles, was du willst."

"You mean like telling her a little bit of poetry or   72.1
something?"
"Du meinst, ich soll ihr ein kleines Gedicht vortragen oder
so?"

"That's it," said Rabbit. "Splendid. Now come along."   73.1
"Das war's," sagte Rabbit. "Prächtig. Und jetzt komm mit."

So they all went out to look for Kanga.   74.1
Also gingen sie alle los, um Kanga zu suchen.

Kanga and Roo were spending a quiet afternoon in a   75.1
sandy part of the Forest.
Kanga und Roo verbrachten einen ruhigen Nachmittag in
einem sandigen Teil des Waldes.

Baby Roo was practising very small jumps in the sand,   75.2
and falling down mouse-holes and climbing out of
them, and Kanga was fidgeting about and saying
Der kleine Ruh übte ganz kleine Sprünge im Sand, fiel
in Mäuselöcher und kletterte wieder heraus, und Kanga
zappelte herum und sagte,

184

75.3 "Just one more jump, dear, and then we must go home."

"Nur noch einen Sprung, Schatz, dann müssen wir nach Hause gehen."

75.4 And at that moment who should come stumping up the hill but Pooh.

Und wer kam in diesem Moment den Hügel hinaufgestapft, außer Puuh.

77.1 "Good afternoon, Kanga."

"Guten Tag, Kanga."

78.1 "Good afternoon, Pooh."

"Guten Tag, Puuh."

79.1 "Look at me jumping,"

"Schau, wie ich hüpfe,"

79.2 squeaked Roo, and fell into another mouse-hole.

quietschte Ruh und fiel in ein weiteres Mauseloch.

80.1 "Hallo, Roo, my little fellow!"

"Hallo, Ruh, mein kleiner Freund!"

"We were just going home," said Kanga. 81.1
"Wir wollten gerade nach Hause gehen," sagte Kanga.

"Good afternoon, Rabbit. Good afternoon, Piglet." 81.2
"Guten Tag, Kaninchen. Guten Tag, Ferkel."

Rabbit and Piglet, who had now come up from the 82.1
other side of the hill, said
Hase und Ferkel, die inzwischen von der anderen Seite des
Hügels heraufgekommen waren, sagten

"Good afternoon," and "Hallo, Roo," 82.2
"Guten Tag" und "Hallo, Ruh,"

and Roo asked them to look at him jumping, so they 82.3
stayed and looked.
und Ruh bat sie, ihm beim Springen zuzusehen, und so
blieben sie und schauten.

And Kanga looked too ... 83.1
Und Kanga sah auch ...

"Oh, Kanga," 84.1
"Oh, Kanga,"

said Pooh, after Rabbit had winked at him twice, 84.2
sagte Puuh, nachdem Kaninchen ihm zweimal zugeblinzelt
hatte,

"I don't know if you are interested in Poetry at all?" 84.3
"ich weiß nicht, ob du überhaupt an Poesie interessiert
bist?"

"Hardly at all," said Kanga. 85.1
"Überhaupt nicht," sagte Kanga.

186

86.1 "Oh!" said Pooh.
"Oh!" sagte Puuh.

87.1 "Roo, dear, just one more jump and then we must go home."
"Ruh, Schatz, nur noch ein Sprung, dann müssen wir nach Hause."

88.1 There was a short silence while Roo fell down another mouse-hole.
Es herrschte eine kurze Stille, während Roo in ein weiteres Mauseloch fiel.

89.1 "Go on,"
"Geh schon,"

89.2 said Rabbit in a loud whisper behind his paw.
sagte Kaninchen laut flüsternd hinter seiner Pfote.

90.1 "Talking of Poetry," said Pooh,
"Apropos Poesie," sagte Pooh,

90.2 "I made up a little piece as I was coming along.
"ich habe mir ein kleines Stück ausgedacht, während ich unterwegs war.

90.3 It went like this. Er — now let me see —— "
Es ging ungefähr so. Äh, lass mich mal sehen …"

91.1 "Fancy!" said Kanga. "Now Roo, dear —— "
"Fantastisch!" sagte Kanga. "Jetzt Roo, mein Lieber …"

92.1 "You'll like this piece of poetry," said Rabbit.
"Dieses Gedicht wird dir gefallen," sagte Rabbit.

"You'll love it," said Piglet.   93.1

"Es wird dir gefallen," sagte Ferkel.

"You must listen very carefully," said Rabbit.   94.1

"Du musst sehr genau zuhören," sagte Rabbit.

"So as not to miss any of it," said Piglet.   95.1

"Um nichts zu verpassen," sagte Ferkel.

"Oh, yes," said Kanga, but she still looked at Baby   96.1
Roo.

"Oh ja," sagte Kanga, aber sie schaute immer noch zu Baby
Ruh.

"How did it go, Pooh?" said Rabbit.   97.1

"Wie ist es gelaufen, Puuh?" fragte Rabbit.

Pooh gave a little cough and began.   98.1

Pooh hustete ein wenig und begann.

LINES WRITTEN BY A BEAR OF VERY LITTLE   99.1
BRAIN

ZEILEN, GESCHRIEBEN VON EINEM BÄREN MIT SEHR
WENIG HIRN

On Monday, when the sun is hot   100.1

Am Montag, wenn die Sonne heiß ist

I wonder to myself a lot: 101.1

Das frage ich mich auch oft:

102.1 "Now is it true, or is it not,
"Stimmt es nun oder nicht?

103.1 "That what is which and which is what?"
"Was ist was und was ist was?"

104.1 On Tuesday, when it hails and snows,
Am Dienstag, wenn es hagelt und schneit,

105.1 The feeling on me grows and grows
Das Gefühl in mir wächst und wächst

106.1 That hardly anybody knows
Was kaum jemand weiß

107.1 If those are these or these are those.
Wenn das diese sind oder diese jene sind.

108.1 On Wednesday, when the sky is blue,
Am Mittwoch, wenn der Himmel blau ist,

109.1 And I have nothing else to do,
Und ich habe nichts anderes zu tun,

110.1 I sometimes wonder if it's true
Ich frage mich manchmal, ob es wahr ist

111.1 That who is what and what is who.
Das Wer ist was und das Was ist wer.

112.1 On Thursday, when it starts to freeze
Am Donnerstag, wenn es zu frieren beginnt

And hoar-frost twinkles on the trees, 113.1
Und Raureif glitzert auf den Bäumen,

How very readily one sees 114.1
Wie leicht man sieht

That these are whose - but whose are these? 115.1
Das sind sie - aber wer sind sie?

On Friday —— 116.1
Am Freitag ...

"Yes, it is, isn't it?" 117.1
"Ja, das ist es, nicht wahr?"

said Kanga, not waiting to hear what happened on 117.2
Friday.
sagte Kanga, ohne abzuwarten, was am Freitag geschah.

"Just one more jump, Roo, dear, and then we really 117.3
must be going."
"Nur noch ein Sprung, Ruh, mein Lieber, und dann müssen
wir wirklich los."

119.1 Rabbit gave Pooh a hurrying-up sort of nudge.
Kaninchen gab Puuh einen eiligen Schubs.

120.1 "Talking of Poetry," said Pooh quickly,
"Apropos Poesie," sagte Pooh schnell,

120.2 "have you ever noticed that tree right over there?"
"ist dir jemals der Baum dort drüben aufgefallen?"

121.1 "Where?" said Kanga. "Now, Roo —— "
"Wo?" sagte Kanga. "Also, Ruh …"

122.1 "Right over there," said Pooh, pointing behind
Kanga's back.
"Da drüben," sagte Pooh und deutete hinter Kangas
Rücken.

123.1 "No," said Kanga.
"Nein," sagte Kanga.

123.2 "Now jump in, Roo, dear, and we'll go home."
"Jetzt spring rein, Ruh, Schatz, und wir gehen nach
Hause."

124.1 "You ought to look at that tree right over there," said
Rabbit.
"Du solltest dir den Baum dort drüben ansehen," sagte
Rabbit.

124.2 "Shall I lift you in, Roo?"
"Soll ich dich hineinheben, Ruh?"

124.3 And he picked up Roo in his paws.
Und er hob Ruh in seine Pfoten.

"I can see a bird in it from here," said Pooh. 125.1
"Ich kann von hier aus einen Vogel darin sehen," sagte
Puuh.

"Or is it a fish?" 125.2
"Oder ist es ein Fisch?"

"You ought to see that bird from here," said Rabbit. 126.1
"Den Vogel müsstest du von hier aus sehen," sagte Rabbit.

"Unless it's a fish." 126.2
"Es sei denn, es ist ein Fisch."

"It isn't a fish, it's a bird," said Piglet. 127.1
"Das ist kein Fisch, das ist ein Vogel," sagte Ferkel.

"So it is," said Rabbit. 128.1
"So ist es," sagte Rabbit.

"Is it a starling or a blackbird?" said Pooh. 129.1
"Ist es ein Star oder eine Amsel?" fragte Puuh.

"That's the whole question," said Rabbit. 130.1
"Das ist die ganze Frage," sagte der Hase.

"Is it a blackbird or a starling?" 130.2
"Ist es eine Amsel oder ein Star?"

And then at last Kanga did turn her head to look. 131.1
Und dann drehte Kanga endlich ihren Kopf, um zu
schauen.

131.2 **And the moment that her head was turned, Rabbit said in a loud voice**

Und in dem Moment, als sie den Kopf drehte, sagte der Hase mit lauter Stimme

131.3 **"In you go, Roo!"**

"Rein mit dir, Ruh!"

131.4 **and in jumped Piglet into Kanga's pocket, and off scampered Rabbit, with Roo in his paws, as fast as he could.**

und das Ferkel sprang in Kangas Tasche, und der Hase huschte mit Ruh in seinen Pfoten davon, so schnell er konnte.

132.1 **"Why, where's Rabbit?" said Kanga, turning round again.**

"Wo ist denn Rabbit?" fragte Kanga und drehte sich wieder um.

132.2 **"Are you all right, Roo, dear?"**

"Geht es dir gut, Ruh, Liebes?"

133.1 **Piglet made a squeaky Roo-noise from the bottom of Kanga's pocket.**

Ferkel machte ein quietschendes Ruh-Geräusch vom Boden von Kangas Tasche.

134.1 **"Rabbit had to go away," said Pooh.**

"Der Hase musste weg," sagte Puuh.

134.2 **"I think he thought of something he had to go and see about suddenly."**

"Ich glaube, ihm ist plötzlich etwas eingefallen, das er erledigen muss."

"And Piglet?" 135.1

"Und Ferkel?"

"I think Piglet thought of something at the same 136.1
time.

"Ich glaube, Ferkel hat zur gleichen Zeit an etwas gedacht.

Suddenly." 136.2

Plötzlich."

"Well, we must be getting home," said Kanga. 138.1

"Nun, wir müssen nach Hause," sagte Kanga.

"Good-bye, Pooh." 138.2

"Auf Wiedersehen, Puuh."

And in three large jumps she was gone. 138.3

Und mit drei großen Sprüngen war sie weg.

Pooh looked after her as she went. 139.1

Puuh schaute ihr nach, als sie ging.

"I wish I could jump like that," he thought. 140.1

"Ich wünschte, ich könnte so springen," dachte er.

140.2 "Some can and some can't. That's how it is."
"Manche können es und manche nicht. So ist das nun mal."

141.1 But there were moments when Piglet wished that
Kanga couldn't.
Aber es gab Momente, in denen Ferkel sich wünschte, dass
Kanga das nicht könnte.

141.2 Often, when he had had a long walk home through
the Forest, he had wished that he were a bird;
Oft, wenn er einen langen Spaziergang durch den Wald
nach Hause gemacht hatte, hatte er sich gewünscht, ein
Vogel zu sein;

141.3 but now he thought jerkily to himself at the bottom
of Kanga's pocket,
aber jetzt dachte er ruckartig an sich selbst, an den Boden
von Kangas Tasche,

142.1 this take
diese Aufnahme

143.1 "If is shall really to
"Wenn das wirklich so sein soll

144.1 flying I never it."
Ich fliege es nie."

145.1 And as he went up in the air he said, "Ooooooo!"
Und als er in die Luft ging, sagte er, "Ooooooo!"

145.2 and as he came down he said, "Ow!" And he was
saying,
und als er herunterkam, sagte er, "Au!" Und er sagte,

"Ooooooo-ow, Ooooooo-ow, Ooooooo- ow" 145.3

"Ooooooo-ow, Ooooooo-ow, Ooooooo- ow"

all the way to Kanga's house. 145.4

auf dem ganzen Weg zu Kangas Haus.

Of course as soon as Kanga unbuttoned her pocket, 146.1
she saw what had happened.

Als Kanga ihre Tasche aufknöpfte, sah sie natürlich sofort,
was passiert war.

Just for a moment, she thought she was frightened, 146.2
and then she knew she wasn't; for she felt quite sure
that Christopher Robin would never let any harm
happen to Roo.

Einen Moment lang dachte sie, sie hätte Angst, aber dann
wusste sie, dass sie es nicht war, denn sie war sich sicher,
dass Christopher Robin Roo nie etwas zustoßen würde.

So she said to herself, 146.3

Also sagte sie zu sich selbst,

"If they are having a joke with me, 146.4

"Wenn sie sich einen Scherz mit mir erlauben,

I will have a joke with them." 146.5

werde ich mir einen Scherz mit ihnen erlauben."

148.1 "Now then, Roo, dear," she said,
"So, Ruh, mein Lieber," sagte sie,

148.2 as she took Piglet out of her pocket. "Bed- time."
als sie Ferkel aus ihrer Tasche nahm. "Schlafenszeit."

149.1 "Aha!" said Piglet,
"Aha!" sagte Ferkel,

149.2 as well as he could after his Terrifying Journey.
so gut es nach seiner schrecklichen Reise eben konnte.

149.3 But it wasn't a very good "Aha!"
Aber es war kein besonders gutes "Aha!"

149.4 and Kanga didn't seem to understand what it meant.
und Kanga schien nicht zu verstehen, was es bedeutete.

150.1 "Bath first," said Kanga in a cheerful voice.
"Zuerst das Bad," sagte Kanga mit fröhlicher Stimme.

151.1 "Aha!"
"Aha!"

151.2 said Piglet again, looking round anxiously for the
others.
sagte Ferkel wieder und sah sich ängstlich nach den
anderen um.

151.3 But the others weren't there.
Aber die anderen waren nicht da.

Rabbit was playing with Baby Roo in his own house, 151.4
and feeling more fond of him every minute, and
Pooh, who had decided to be a Kanga, was still at
the sandy place on the top of the Forest, practising
jumps.

Kaninchen spielte mit dem kleinen Ruh in seinem eigenen
Haus und mochte ihn von Minute zu Minute mehr, und
Puuh, der beschlossen hatte, ein Kanga zu werden, war
immer noch an der sandigen Stelle auf dem Gipfel des
Waldes und übte Sprünge.

"I am not at all sure," 153.1

"Ich bin mir gar nicht so sicher,"

said Kanga in a thoughtful voice, 153.2

sagte Kanga mit nachdenklicher Stimme,

"that it wouldn't be a good idea to have a cold bath 153.3
this evening.

"ob es nicht eine gute Idee wäre, heute Abend ein kaltes Bad
zu nehmen.

Would you like that, Roo, dear?" 153.4

Hättest du das gern, Ruh, meine Liebe?"

154.1 **Piglet, who had never been really fond of baths, shuddered a long indignant shudder, and said in as brave a voice as he could:**

Ferkel, das noch nie gerne gebadet hatte, erschauderte lange empört und sagte mit so tapferer Stimme, wie es konnte:

155.1 **"Kanga, I see that the time has come to spleak painly."**

"Kanga, ich sehe, dass die Zeit gekommen ist, schmerzhaft zu lecken."

156.1 **"Funny little Roo," said Kanga,**

"Komischer kleiner Ruh," sagte Kanga,

156.2 **as she got the bath-water ready.**

während sie das Badewasser bereitete.

157.1 **"I am not Roo," said Piglet loudly. "I am Piglet!"**

"Ich bin nicht Ruh," sagte Ferkel laut. "Ich bin Ferkel!"

158.1 **"Yes, dear, yes," said Kanga soothingly.**

"Ja, Liebes, ja," sagte Kanga beruhigend.

158.2 **"And imitating Piglet's voice too!**

"Und er ahmt auch noch Ferkels Stimme nach!

158.3 **So clever of him," she went on,**

Wie schlau von ihm," fuhr sie fort,

158.4 **as she took a large bar of yellow soap out of the cupboard.**

während sie ein großes Stück gelbe Seife aus dem Schrank holte.

"What will he be doing next?"   158.5
"Was wird er als nächstes tun?"

"Can't you see?" shouted Piglet.   159.1
"Kannst du nicht sehen?" rief Ferkel.

"Haven't you got eyes? Look at me!"   159.2
"Hast du keine Augen im Kopf? Sieh mich an!"

"I am looking, Roo, dear," said Kanga rather severely.   160.1
"Ich schaue, Ruh, mein Lieber," sagte Kanga ziemlich
streng.

"And you know what I told you yesterday about   160.2
making faces.
"Und du weißt ja, was ich dir gestern über das
Grimassenschneiden gesagt habe.

If you go on making faces like Piglet's,   160.3
Wenn du weiter solche Grimassen schneidest wie Ferkel,

you will grow up to look like Piglet -   160.4
wirst du bald so aussehen wie Ferkel -

and then think how sorry you will be.   160.5
und dann wird es dir leid tun.

Now then, into the bath, and don't let me have to   160.6
speak to you about it again."
Und jetzt ab in die Wanne, und lass mich nicht noch einmal
mit dir darüber reden."

161.1 **Before he knew where he was, Piglet was in the bath, and Kanga was scrubbing him firmly with a large lathery flannel.**

Bevor er wusste, wo er war, saß Ferkel in der Badewanne, und Kanga schrubbte es mit einem großen, schaumigen Waschlappen ab.

163.1 **"Ow!" cried Piglet. "Let me out! I'm Piglet!"**

"Au!" schrie Ferkel. "Lass mich raus! Ich bin Ferkel!"

164.1 **"Don't open the mouth, dear, or the soap goes in,"**

"Mach den Mund nicht auf, Liebes, sonst geht die Seife rein,"

164.2 **said Kanga. "There! What did I tell you?"**

sagte Kanga. "So! Was habe ich dir gesagt?"

165.1 **"You — you — you did it on purpose," spluttered Piglet,**

"Du, du, du hast es absichtlich getan," stotterte Ferkel,

165.2 **as soon as he could speak again ...**

sobald es wieder sprechen konnte ...

and then accidentally had another mouthful of
lathery flannel.

165.3

und hatte dann versehentlich wieder den Mund voll mit
schaumigem Flanell.

"That's right, dear, don't say anything,"

166.1

"So ist's recht, Liebes, sag nichts,"

said Kanga, and in another minute Piglet was out of
the bath, and being rubbed dry with a towel.

166.2

sagte Kanga, und in einer Minute war Ferkel aus dem Bad
und wurde mit einem Handtuch trocken gerieben.

"Now," said Kanga, "there's your medicine,

167.1

"Jetzt," sagte Kanga, "gibt es deine Medizin,

and then bed."

167.2

und dann geht es ins Bett."

"W-w-what medicine?" said Piglet.

168.1

"W-w-welche Medizin?" sagte Ferkel.

"To make you grow big and strong, dear.

169.1

"Damit du groß und stark wirst, mein Schatz.

You don't want to grow up small and weak like Piglet,
do you?

169.2

Du willst doch nicht klein und schwach werden wie Ferkel,
oder?

Well, then!"

169.3

Na, dann!"

170.1 At that moment there was a knock at the door.

In diesem Moment klopfte es an der Tür.

171.1 "Come in," said Kanga, and in came Christopher
Robin.

"Komm herein," sagte Kanga, und Christopher Robin kam
herein.

173.1 "Christopher Robin, Christopher Robin!" cried
Piglet.

"Christopher Robin, Christopher Robin!" rief Ferkel.

173.2 "Tell Kanga who I am! She keeps saying I'm Roo.

"Sag Kanga, wer ich bin! Sie sagt immer, ich sei Ruh.

173.3 I'm not Roo, am I?"

Ich bin aber nicht Ruh, oder?"

174.1 Christopher Robin looked at him very carefully, and
shook his head.

Christopher Robin schaute ihn sehr genau an und
schüttelte den Kopf.

175.1 "You can't be Roo," he said,

"Du kannst nicht Roo sein," sagte er,

"because I've just seen Roo playing in Rabbit's
house."

175.2

"denn ich habe Roo gerade in Rabbits Haus spielen sehen."

"Well!" said Kanga. "Fancy that!

176.1

"Nun!" sagte Kanga. "Stell dir das vor!

Fancy my making a mistake like that."

176.2

Dass ich so einen Fehler mache."

"There you are!" said Piglet. "I told you so.

177.1

"Da bist du ja!" sagte Ferkel. "Ich habe es dir gesagt.

I'm Piglet."

177.2

Ich bin Ferkel."

Christopher Robin shook his head again.

178.1

Christopher Robin schüttelte wieder den Kopf.

"Oh, you're not Piglet," he said.

179.1

"Oh, du bist nicht Ferkel," sagte er.

"I know Piglet well, and he's quite a different colour."

179.2

"Ich kenne Ferkel gut, und es hat eine ganz andere Farbe."

180.1 Piglet began to say that this was because he had just
had a bath, and then he thought that perhaps he
wouldn't say that, and as he opened his mouth to say
something else, Kanga slipped the medicine spoon in,
and then patted him on the back and told him that it
was really quite a nice taste when you got used to it.

Ferkel wollte gerade sagen, dass es daran lag, dass er gerade
gebadet hatte, aber dann dachte es, dass es das vielleicht
nicht sagen sollte, und als es den Mund öffnete, um etwas
anderes zu sagen, schob Kanga den Medizinlöffel hinein,
klopfte ihm auf die Schulter und sagte, dass es wirklich
sehr gut schmeckt, wenn man sich daran gewöhnt.

181.1 "I knew it wasn't Piglet," said Kanga.

"Ich wusste, dass es nicht Ferkel war," sagte Kanga.

181.2 "I wonder who it can be."

"Ich frage mich, wer es sein könnte."

182.1 "Perhaps it's some relation of Pooh's,"

"Vielleicht ist es ein Verwandter von Pooh,"

182.2 said Christopher Robin.

sagte Christopher Robin.

182.3 "What about a nephew or an uncle or something?"

"Wie wäre es mit einem Neffen oder einem Onkel oder so?"

183.1 Kanga agreed that this was probably what it was, and
said that they would have to call it by some name.

Kanga stimmte zu, dass es sich wahrscheinlich darum
handelte, und sagte, dass sie ihm einen Namen geben
müssten.

184.1 "I shall call it Pootel," said Christopher Robin.

"Ich werde ihn Pootel nennen," sagte Christopher Robin.

"Henry Pootel for short."   184.2

"Kurz: Henry Pootel."

And just when it was decided,   185.1

Und gerade als die Entscheidung gefallen war,

Henry Pootel wriggled out of Kanga's arms and   185.2
jumped to the ground.

riss sich Henry Pootel aus Kangas Armen und sprang zu
Boden.

To his great joy Christopher Robin had left the door   185.3
open.

Zu seiner großen Freude hatte Christopher Robin die Tür
offen gelassen.

Never had Henry Pootel Piglet run so fast as he ran   185.4
then, and he didn't stop running until he had got
quite close to his house.

Noch nie war Henry Pootel Piglet so schnell gerannt wie in
diesem Moment, und er hörte nicht auf zu rennen, bis er
ganz in der Nähe seines Hauses war.

But when he was a hundred yards away he stopped   185.5
running, and rolled the rest of the way home, so as to
get his own nice comfortable colour again ...

Aber als er hundert Meter entfernt war, hörte er auf zu
rennen und rollte den Rest des Weges nach Hause, um sich
wieder eine schöne, bequeme Farbe zuzulegen ...

187.1 **So Kanga and Roo stayed in the Forest.**

Also blieben Kanga und Ruh im Wald.

187.2 **And every Tuesday Roo spent the day with his great
friend Rabbit, and every Tuesday Kanga spent the
day with her great friend Pooh, teaching him to jump,
and every Tuesday Piglet spent the day with his great
friend Christopher Robin.**

Und jeden Dienstag verbrachte Ruh den Tag mit seinem
großen Freund Kaninchen, und jeden Dienstag verbrachte
Kanga den Tag mit ihrem großen Freund Puuh und brachte
ihm das Springen bei, und jeden Dienstag verbrachte
Ferkel den Tag mit seinem großen Freund Christopher
Robin.

187.3 **So they were all happy again.**

So waren sie alle wieder glücklich.

CHAPTER VIII · IN WHICH CHRISTOPHER ROBIN LEADS AN EXPOTITION TO THE NORTH POLE

KAPITEL VIII · IN DEM CHRISTOPHER
ROBIN EINE EXPEDITION ZUM NORDPOL
ANFÜHRT

1.1 One fine day Pooh had stumped up to the top of the
Forest to see if his friend Christopher Robin was
interested in Bears at all.

Eines schönen Tages war Puuh auf den Gipfel des Waldes
gestiegen, um zu sehen, ob sein Freund Christopher Robin
sich überhaupt für Bären interessierte.

1.2 At breakfast that morning (a simple meal of
marmalade spread lightly over a honeycomb or two)
he had suddenly thought of a new song.

Beim Frühstück an diesem Morgen (eine einfache Mahlzeit
aus Marmelade, die leicht auf ein oder zwei Honigwaben
gestrichen wurde) war ihm plötzlich ein neues Lied
eingefallen.

It began like this: 1.3
Es begann wie folgt:

"   2.1
"

Sing Ho! for the life of a Bear.   3.1
Sing Ho! für das Leben eines Bären.

"   4.1
"

When he had got as far as this, he scratched his head, 5.1
and thought to himself
Als er so weit gekommen war, kratzte er sich am Kopf und
dachte sich

"That's a very good start for a song,   5.2
"Das ist ein sehr guter Anfang für ein Lied,

but what about the second line?" He tried singing   5.3
"Ho,"
aber was ist mit der zweiten Zeile?" Er versuchte "Ho"

two or three times, but it didn't seem to help.   5.4
zwei - oder dreimal zu singen, aber es schien nicht zu
helfen.

"Perhaps it would be better," he thought,   5.5
"Vielleicht wäre es besser," dachte er,

"if I sang Hi for the life of a Bear."   5.6
"wenn ich Hi for the life of a Bear singen würde."

So he sang it ...but it wasn't. "Very well, then,"   5.7
Also sang er es ...aber es half nicht. "Nun gut,"

210

5.8 **he said,**

sagte er,

5.9 **"I shall sing that first line twice, and perhaps if I sing it very quickly, I shall find myself singing the third and fourth lines before I have time to think of them, and that will be a Good Song.**

"ich werde die erste Zeile zweimal singen, und vielleicht, wenn ich sie sehr schnell singe, werde ich mich dabei ertappen, wie ich die dritte und vierte Zeile singe, bevor ich Zeit habe, an sie zu denken, und das wird ein gutes Lied sein.

5.10 **Now then:"**

Nun denn:"

6.1 **Sing Ho! for the life of a Bear!**

Sing Ho! für das Leben eines Bären!

7.1 **Sing Ho! for the life of a Bear!**

Sing Ho! für das Leben eines Bären!

8.1 **I don't much mind if it rains or snows,**

Es macht mir nicht viel aus, wenn es regnet oder schneit,

9.1 **'Cos I've got a lot of honey on my nice new nose,**

Denn ich habe eine Menge Honig auf meiner schönen neuen Nase,

10.1 **I don't much care if it snows or thaws,**

Es ist mir ziemlich egal, ob es schneit oder taut,

'Cos I've got a lot of honey on my nice clean paws! 11.1

Denn ich habe eine Menge Honig an meinen schönen
sauberen Pfoten!

Sing Ho! for a Bear! 12.1

Sing Ho! für einen Bären!

Sing Ho! for a Pooh! 13.1

Sing Ho! für ein Pooh!

And I'll have a little something in an hour or two! 14.1

Und in ein oder zwei Stunden habe ich eine Kleinigkeit!

He was so pleased with this song that he sang it all the 15.1
way to the top of the Forest,

Dieses Lied gefiel ihm so gut, dass er es bis zum Ende des
Waldes sang,

"and if I go on singing it much longer," he thought, 15.2

"und wenn ich es noch länger singe," dachte er,

"it will be time for the little something, 15.3

"wird es Zeit für das kleine Etwas,

and then the last line won't be true." 15.4

und dann ist die letzte Zeile nicht mehr wahr."

So he turned it into a hum instead. 15.5

Also verwandelte er sie stattdessen in ein Summen.

Christopher Robin was sitting outside his door, 16.1
putting on his Big Boots.

Christopher Robin saß vor seiner Tür und zog seine großen
Stiefel an.

212

16.2 As soon as he saw the Big Boots, Pooh knew that an
Adventure was going to happen, and he brushed
the honey off his nose with the back of his paw, and
spruced himself up as well as he could, so as to look
Ready for Anything.

Sobald er die großen Stiefel sah, wusste Puuh, dass ein
Abenteuer bevorstand, und er wischte sich mit dem Rücken
seiner Pfote den Honig von der Nase und putzte sich so gut
wie möglich heraus, um für alles bereit zu sein.

17.1 "Good-morning, Christopher Robin," he called out.

"Guten Morgen, Christopher Robin," rief er.

18.1 "Hallo, Pooh Bear. I can't get this boot on."

"Hallo, Puuh-Bär. Ich kriege den Stiefel nicht an."

19.1 "That's bad," said Pooh.

"Das ist schlecht," sagte Pooh.

20.1 "Do you think you could very kindly lean against me,
'cos I keep pulling so hard that I fall over backwards."

"Könntest du dich bitte gegen mich lehnen, denn ich ziehe
immer so stark, dass ich nach hinten umkippe."

Pooh sat down, dug his feet into the ground, and
pushed hard against Christopher Robin's back, and
Christopher Robin pushed hard against his, and
pulled and pulled at his boot until he had got it on.

22.1

Puuh setzte sich hin, grub seine Füße in den Boden und
drückte kräftig gegen Christopher Robins Rücken, und
Christopher Robin drückte kräftig gegen seinen und zog
und zog an seinem Stiefel, bis er ihn angezogen hatte.

"And that's that," said Pooh.

23.1

"Das war's dann," sagte Pooh.

"What do we do next?"

23.2

"Was machen wir als nächstes?"

"We are all going on an Expedition," said Christopher
Robin,

24.1

"Wir gehen alle auf eine Expedition," sagte Christopher
Robin,

as he got up and brushed himself. "Thank you, Pooh."

24.2

als er aufstand und sich putzte. "Danke, Puuh."

"Going on an Expotition?" said Pooh eagerly.

25.1

"Du gehst auf eine Expedition?" fragte Puuh eifrig.

"I don't think I've ever been on one of those.

25.2

"Ich glaube, ich war noch nie auf so einer.

Where are we going to on this Expotition?"

25.3

Wohin gehen wir auf dieser Expedition?"

"Expedition, silly old Bear. It's got an 'x' in it."

26.1

"Expedition, dummer alter Bär. Da ist ein 'X' drin."

27.1 "Oh!" said Pooh. "I know."
"Oh!" sagte Puuh. "Ich weiß."

27.2 But he didn't really.
Aber er wusste es nicht wirklich.

28.1 "We're going to discover the North Pole."
"Wir werden den Nordpol entdecken."

29.1 "Oh!" said Pooh again. "What is the North Pole?" he
asked.
"Oh!" sagte Puuh wieder. "Was ist der Nordpol?" fragte er.

30.1 "It's just a thing you discover,"
"Das ist nur eine Sache, die man entdeckt,"

30.2 said Christopher Robin carelessly,
sagte Christopher Robin nachlässig,

30.3 not being quite sure himself.
da er sich selbst nicht ganz sicher war.

31.1 "Oh! I see," said Pooh.
"Oh! Ich verstehe," sagte Pooh.

31.2 "Are bears any good at discovering it?"
"Sind Bären gut darin, sie zu entdecken?"

32.1 "Of course they are. And Rabbit and Kanga and all of
you.
"Natürlich sind sie das. Und Kaninchen und Kanga und ihr
alle.

32.2 It's an Expedition.
Es ist eine Expedition.

That's what an Expedition means.   32.3
Das ist es, was eine Expedition bedeutet.

A long line of everybody.   32.4
Eine lange Reihe von allen.

You'd better tell the others to get ready, while I see if   32.5
my gun's all right.
Sag den anderen, sie sollen sich bereit machen, während
ich nachsehe, ob mein Gewehr in Ordnung ist.

And we must all bring Provisions."   32.6
Und wir müssen alle Proviant mitnehmen."

"Bring what?"   33.1
"Was mitbringen?"

"Things to eat."   34.1
"Dinge zum Essen."

"Oh!" said Pooh happily.   35.1
"Oh!" sagte Puuh fröhlich.

"I thought you said Provisions. I'll go and tell them."   35.2
"Ich dachte, du sagtest Proviant. Ich gehe und sage es
ihnen."

And he stumped off.   35.3
Und er stapfte los.

The first person he met was Rabbit.   36.1
Die erste Person, die er traf, war Rabbit.

38.1 "Hallo, Rabbit," he said, "is that you?"
"Hallo, Hase," sagte er, "bist du das?"

39.1 "Let's pretend it isn't," said Rabbit,
"Tun wir so, als ob es nicht so wäre," sagte Rabbit,

39.2 "and see what happens."
"und schauen, was passiert."

40.1 "I've got a message for you."
"Ich habe eine Nachricht für Sie."

41.1 "I'll give it to him."
"Ich werde es ihm geben."

42.1 "We're all going on an Expotition with Christopher
Robin!"
"Wir gehen alle auf eine Expedition mit Christopher
Robin!"

43.1 "What is it when we're on it?"
"Was ist das, wenn wir dabei sind?"

"A sort of boat, I think," said Pooh. 44.1
"Eine Art Boot, glaube ich," sagte Puuh.

"Oh! that sort." 45.1
"Oh! diese Art."

"Yes. And we're going to discover a Pole or 46.1
something.
"Ja. Und wir werden einen Pol oder so etwas entdecken.

Or was it a Mole? 46.2
Oder war es ein Maulwurf?

Anyhow we're going to discover it." 46.3
Wie auch immer, wir werden ihn entdecken."

"We are, are we?" said Rabbit. 47.1
"Das tun wir doch, oder?" sagte Kaninchen.

"Yes. And we've got to bring Pro — things to eat 48.1
with us.
"Ja. Und wir müssen Pro — Dinge zum Essen mitbringen.

In case we want to eat them. 48.2
Für den Fall, dass wir sie essen wollen.

Now I'm going down to Piglet's. Tell Kanga, will 48.3
you?"
Ich gehe jetzt runter zu Ferkel. Sag Kanga Bescheid, ja?"

He left Rabbit and hurried down to Piglet's house. 49.1
Er verließ den Hasen und eilte zum Haus des Ferkels
hinunter.

49.2 The Piglet was sitting on the ground at the door
of his house blowing happily at a dandelion, and
wondering whether it would be this year, next year,
sometime or never.

Das Ferkel saß auf dem Boden vor der Tür seines Hauses
und pustete fröhlich auf einen Löwenzahn und fragte sich,
ob es dieses Jahr, nächstes Jahr, irgendwann oder nie sein
würde.

49.3 He had just discovered that it would be never, and
was trying to remember what

Es hatte gerade herausgefunden, dass es nie sein würde,
und versuchte sich zu erinnern, was

49.4 "it"

"es"

49.5 was, and hoping it wasn't anything nice, when Pooh
came up.

war, und hoffte, dass es nichts Schönes war, als Puuh
auftauchte.

51.1 "Oh! Piglet," said Pooh excitedly,

"Oh! Ferkel," sagte Puuh aufgeregt,

"we're going on an Expotition, all of us, with things
to eat. 51.2

"wir gehen auf eine Expedition, wir alle, mit Dingen zum
Essen.

To discover something." 51.3

Um etwas zu entdecken."

"To discover what?" said Piglet anxiously. 52.1

"Um was zu entdecken?" fragte Ferkel ängstlich.

"Oh! just something." 53.1

"Oh! Nur etwas."

"Nothing fierce?" 54.1

"Nichts Wildes?"

"Christopher Robin didn't say anything about fierce. 55.1

"Christopher Robin hat nichts von heftig gesagt.

He just said it had an 'x'." 55.2

Er hat nur gesagt, dass es ein 'X' hat."

"It isn't their necks I mind," 56.1

"Es sind nicht ihre Hälse, die mich stören,"

said Piglet earnestly. "It's their teeth. 56.2

sagte Ferkel ernsthaft. "Es sind ihre Zähne.

But if Christopher Robin is coming I don't mind
anything." 56.3

Aber wenn Christopher Robin kommt, macht mir das
nichts aus."

57.1 In a little while they were all ready at the top of the
Forest,

Nach kurzer Zeit waren sie alle oben im Wald bereit,

57.2 and the Expotition started.

und die Ausstellung begann.

57.3 First came Christopher Robin and Rabbit, then Piglet
and Pooh; then Kanga, with Roo in her pocket, and
Owl; then Eeyore; and, at the end, in a long line, all
Rabbit's friends-and-relations.

Zuerst kamen Christopher Robin und Kaninchen, dann
Ferkel und Puuh, dann Kanga mit Ruh in der Tasche und
Eule, dann I-Aah und am Ende in einer langen Reihe alle
Freunde und Verwandten von Kaninchen.

59.1 "I didn't ask them," explained Rabbit carelessly.

"Ich habe sie nicht gefragt," erklärte Rabbit nachlässig.

59.2 "They just came. They always do.

"Sie sind einfach gekommen. Das tun sie immer.

59.3 They can march at the end, after Eeyore."

Sie können am Ende marschieren, nach I- Aah."

60.1 "What I say," said Eeyore,

"Was ich sage," sagte I-Aah,

"is that it's unsettling.   60.2
"ist, dass es beunruhigend ist.

I didn't want to come on this Expo - what Pooh said.   60.3
Ich wollte nicht auf diese Expo kommen - wie Puuh sagte.

I only came to oblige.   60.4
Ich bin nur gekommen, um zu gehorchen.

But here I am; and if I am the end of the Expo -   60.5
Aber jetzt bin ich hier, und wenn ich das Ende der Expo
bin -

what we're talking about - then let me be the end.   60.6
wovon wir hier sprechen -, dann soll ich das Ende sein.

But if, every time I want to sit down for a little rest, I   60.7
have to brush away half a dozen of Rabbit's smaller
friends-and-relations first, then this isn't an Expo -
Aber wenn ich jedes Mal, wenn ich mich für eine kleine
Pause hinsetzen will, erst ein halbes Dutzend von
Kaninchens kleineren Freunden und Verwandten wegfegen
muss, dann ist das gar keine Expo -

whatever it is -   60.8
was auch immer es ist -

at all, it's simply a Confused Noise. That's what I say. "   60.9
sondern einfach nur ein wirres Geräusch. That's what I
say. "

62.1 **"I see what Eeyore means," said Owl.**
"Ich verstehe, was I-Aah meint," sagte Eule.

62.2 **"If you ask me —— "**
"Wenn du mich fragst ..."

63.1 **"I'm not asking anybody," said Eeyore.**
"Ich frage niemanden," sagte Eeyore.

63.2 **"I'm just telling everybody. We can look for the North Pole,**
"Ich sage es nur allen. Wir können den Nordpol suchen,

63.3 **or we can play**
oder wir können mit dem Endstück eines Ameisennestes

63.4 **'Here we go gathering Nuts and May'**
'Wir sammeln Nüsse und Mai'

63.5 **with the end part of an ant's nest. It's all the same to me."**
spielen. Für mich ist das alles dasselbe."

64.1 **There was a shout from the top of the line.**
Ein Schrei ertönte von der Spitze der Schlange.

"Come on!" called Christopher Robin. 65.1

"Komm schon!" rief Christopher Robin.

"Come on!" called Pooh and Piglet. 66.1

"Komm schon!" riefen Puuh und Ferkel.

"Come on!" called Owl. 67.1

"Komm schon!" rief Eule.

"We're starting," said Rabbit. "I must go." 68.1

"Wir brechen auf," sagte Rabbit. "Ich muss los."

And he hurried off to the front of the Expotition with 68.2
Christopher Robin.

Und er eilte mit Christopher Robin nach vorne zur
Ausstellung.

"All right," said Eeyore. "We're going. 69.1

"In Ordnung," sagte I-Aah. "Wir gehen jetzt.

Only Don't Blame Me." 69.2

Aber gebt mir nicht die Schuld."

So off they all went to discover the Pole. 70.1

Also machten sie sich alle auf den Weg, um den Pol zu
entdecken.

And as they walked, they chattered to each other of 70.2
this and that, all except Pooh, who was making up a
song.

Und während sie gingen, plauderten sie miteinander über
dies und das, alle außer Puuh, der sich ein Lied ausdachte.

71.1 "This is the first verse," he said to Piglet,
"Das ist die erste Strophe," sagte er zu Ferkel,

71.2 when he was ready with it.
als er sie fertig hatte.

72.1 "First verse of what?"
"Erste Strophe von was?"

73.1 "My song."
"Mein Lied."

74.1 "What song?"
"Welches Lied?"

75.1 "This one."
"Diese hier."

76.1 "Which one?"
"Welche?"

77.1 "Well, if you listen, Piglet, you'll hear it."
"Nun, wenn du zuhörst, Ferkel, wirst du es hören."

78.1 "How do you know I'm not listening?"
"Woher wissen Sie, dass ich nicht zuhöre?"

79.1 Pooh couldn't answer that one, so he began to sing.
Darauf konnte Puuh nicht antworten, also begann er zu
singen.

They all went off to discover the Pole,   80.1
Sie machten sich alle auf, um den Pol zu entdecken,

Owl and Piglet and Rabbit and all;   81.1
Eule und Ferkel und Hase und so weiter;

It's a Thing you Discover, as I've been tole   82.1
Es ist eine Sache, die man entdeckt, wie ich erfahren habe

By Owl and Piglet and Rabbit and all.   83.1
Von Eule und Ferkel und Hase und allen anderen.

Eeyore, Christopher Robin and Pooh   84.1
I-Aah, Christopher Robin und Puuh

And Rabbit's relations all went too — .   85.1
Und die Verwandten von Rabbit sind auch alle weg.

And where the Pole was none of them knew …   86.1
Und wo der Pol war, wusste keiner von ihnen …

Sing Hey! for Owl and Rabbit and all!   87.1
Sing Hey! für Eule und Hase und alle!

"Hush!" said Christopher Robin turning round to   88.1
Pooh,
"Pst!" sagte Christopher Robin und drehte sich zu
Puuh um,

"we're just coming to a Dangerous Place."   88.2
"wir kommen gerade an einen gefährlichen Ort."

90.1 "Hush!" said Pooh turning round quickly to Piglet.

"Pst!" sagte Puuh und drehte sich schnell zu Ferkel um.

91.1 "Hush!" said Piglet to Kanga.

"Still!" sagte Ferkel zu Kanga.

92.1 "Hush!" said Kanga to Owl, while Roo said "Hush!"

"Still!" sagte Kanga zu Eule, und Ruh sagte "Still!"

92.2 several times to himself very quietly.

mehrmals ganz leise zu sich selbst.

93.1 "Hush!" said Owl to Eeyore.

"Still!" sagte Eule zu I-Aah.

94.1 "Hush!"

"Still!"

94.2 said Eeyore in a terrible voice to all Rabbit's friends-
and-relations,

sagte I-Aah mit schrecklicher Stimme zu allen Freunden
und Verwandten des Kaninchens,

94.3 and "Hush!"

und "Still!"

they said hastily to each other all down the line, until
it got to the last one of all.

sagten sie eilig zueinander, die ganze Reihe hinunter, bis es
zum letzten von allen kam.

And the last and smallest friend-and-relation was so
upset to find that the whole Expotition was saying

Und der letzte und kleinste Freund und Verwandter war so
erschrocken, als er merkte, dass die ganze Exposition

"Hush!"

"Still!"

to him, that he buried himself head downwards in
a crack in the ground, and stayed there for two days
until the danger was over, and then went home in
a great hurry, and lived quietly with his Aunt ever-
afterwards.

zu ihm sagte, dass er sich mit dem Kopf nach unten in einer
Erdspalte vergrub und dort zwei Tage lang blieb, bis die
Gefahr vorüber war, und dann in großer Eile nach Hause
ging und von da an ruhig bei seiner Tante lebte.

His name was Alexander Beetle.

Sein Name war Alexander Käfer.

228

96.1 They had come to a stream which twisted and
tumbled between high rocky banks, and Christopher
Robin saw at once how dangerous it was.
Sie waren an einen Bach gekommen, der sich zwischen
hohen Felswänden schlängelte und stürzte, und
Christopher Robin sah sofort, wie gefährlich er war.

97.1 "It's just the place," he explained,
"Es ist genau der richtige Ort," erklärte er,

97.2 "for an Ambush."
"für einen Überfall."

98.1 "What sort of bush?" whispered Pooh to Piglet.
"Was für ein Busch?" flüsterte Puuh zu Ferkel.

98.2 "A gorse- bush?"
"Ein Ginsterbusch?"

99.1 "My dear Pooh," said Owl in his superior way,
"Mein lieber Puuh," sagte Eule in seiner überlegenen Art,

99.2 "don't you know what an Ambush is?"
"weißt du nicht, was ein Hinterhalt ist?"

100.1 "Owl," said Piglet, looking round at him severely,
"Eule," sagte Ferkel und sah ihn streng an,

100.2 "Pooh's whisper was a perfectly private whisper,
"Puuhs Flüstern war ein ganz privates Flüstern,

100.3 and there was no need —— "
und es gab keinen Grund ..."

"An Ambush," said Owl, "is a sort of Surprise."   101.1
"Ein Hinterhalt," sagte Eule, "ist eine Art Überraschung."

"So is a gorse-bush sometimes," said Pooh.   102.1
"Das ist ein Ginsterstrauch manchmal auch," sagte Pooh.

"An Ambush, as I was about to explain to Pooh,"   103.1
"Ein Hinterhalt, wie ich Puuh gerade erklären wollte,"

said Piglet, "is a sort of Surprise."   103.2
sagte Ferkel, "ist eine Art von Überraschung."

"If people jump out at you suddenly, that's an   104.1
Ambush,"
"Wenn Leute plötzlich auf dich zustürmen, ist das ein
Hinterhalt,"

said Owl.   104.2
sagte Eule.

"It's an Ambush, Pooh, when people jump at you   105.1
suddenly,"
"Das ist ein Hinterhalt, Puuh, wenn sich die Leute plötzlich
auf dich stürzen,"

explained Piglet.   105.2
erklärt Ferkel.

106.1 Pooh, who now knew what an Ambush was, said that a gorse-bush had sprung at him suddenly one day when he fell off a tree, and he had taken six days to get all the prickles out of himself.

Puuh, der nun wusste, was ein Hinterhalt war, erzählte, dass ihn eines Tages, als er von einem Baum fiel, plötzlich ein Ginsterbusch angesprungen hatte und er sechs Tage gebraucht hatte, um alle Stacheln aus sich herauszubekommen.

107.1 "We are not talking about gorse- bushes,"

"Wir reden hier nicht über Ginsterbüsche,"

107.2 said Owl a little crossly.

sagte Eule ein wenig verärgert.

108.1 "I am," said Pooh.

"Das bin ich," sagte Puuh.

109.1 They were climbing very cautiously up the stream now, going from rock to rock, and after they had gone a little way they came to a place where the banks widened out at each side, so that on each side of the water there was a level strip of grass on which they could sit down and rest.

Sie kletterten nun sehr vorsichtig den Bach hinauf, von Fels zu Fels, und nachdem sie ein Stück weit gegangen waren, kamen sie an eine Stelle, an der sich die Ufer auf beiden Seiten verbreiterten, so dass es auf jeder Seite des Wassers einen ebenen Streifen Gras gab, auf den sie sich setzen und ausruhen konnten.

109.2 As soon as he saw this, Christopher Robin called "Halt!"

Als Christopher Robin dies sah, rief er "Halt!"

and they all sat down and rested. 109.3
und sie setzten sich alle hin und ruhten sich aus.

"I think," said Christopher Robin, 110.1
"Ich denke," sagte Christopher Robin,

"that we ought to eat all our Provisions now, 110.2
"wir sollten jetzt alle unsere Vorräte aufessen,

so that we shan't have so much to carry." 110.3
damit wir nicht so viel zu tragen haben."

"Eat all our what?" said Pooh. 111.1
"Was alles essen?" fragte Pooh.

"All that we've brought," 112.1
"Alles, was wir mitgebracht haben,"

said Piglet, getting to work. 112.2
sagte Ferkel und machte sich an die Arbeit.

"That's a good idea," 113.1
"Das ist eine gute Idee,"

said Pooh, and he got to work too. 113.2
sagte Pooh und machte sich ebenfalls an die Arbeit.

"Have you all got something?" 114.1
"Habt ihr alle etwas?"

asked Christopher Robin with his mouth full. 114.2
fragte Christopher Robin mit vollem Mund.

115.1 "All except me," said Eeyore. "As Usual."
"Alle außer mir," sagte I-Aah. "Wie immer."

115.2 He looked round at them in his melancholy way.
Er schaute sie auf seine melancholische Art an.

115.3 "I suppose none of you are sitting on a thistle by any chance?"
"Ich nehme an, dass keiner von euch zufällig auf einer Distel sitzt?"

116.1 "I believe I am," said Pooh. "Ow!"
"Ich glaube, das bin ich," sagte Puuh. "Au!"

116.2 He got up, and looked behind him. "Yes, I was.
Er stand auf und schaute hinter sich. "Ja, das war ich.

116.3 I thought so."
Dachte ich mir doch."

117.1 "Thank you, Pooh. If you've quite finished with it."
"Danke, Puuh. Wenn du damit fertig bist."

117.2 He moved across to Pooh's place, and began to eat.
Er ging hinüber zu Poohs Platz und begann zu essen.

"It don't do them any Good, you know, sitting on them," 119.1

"Es tut ihnen nicht gut, auf ihnen zu sitzen,"

he went on, as he looked up munching. 119.2

fuhr er fort, während er mümmelnd aufschaute.

"Takes all the Life out of them. Remember that another time, 119.3

"Das nimmt ihnen das ganze Leben. Denkt ein anderes Mal daran,

all of you. 119.4

ihr alle.

A little Consideration, a little Thought for Others, makes all the difference." 119.5

Ein bisschen Rücksichtnahme, ein bisschen Rücksicht auf andere, das macht den Unterschied."

As soon as he had finished his lunch Christopher Robin whispered to Rabbit, and Rabbit said 120.1

Sobald er sein Mittagessen beendet hatte, flüsterte Christopher Robin dem Kaninchen zu, und das Kaninchen sagte

"Yes, yes, of course," 120.2

"Ja, ja, natürlich,"

and they walked a little way up the stream together. 120.3

und sie gingen gemeinsam ein Stück den Bach hinauf.

"I didn't want the others to hear," 121.1

"Ich wollte nicht, dass die anderen das hören,"

121.2 **said Christopher Robin.**
sagte Christopher Robin.

122.1 **"Quite so," said Rabbit, looking important.**
"Ganz recht," sagte Rabbit mit wichtiger Miene.

123.1 **"It's — I wondered — It's only — Rabbit, I suppose
you don't know, What does the North Pole look like?"**
"Ich habe mich gefragt, ob du wohl nicht weißt, wie der
Nordpol aussieht?"

124.1 **"Well," said Rabbit, stroking his whiskers.**
"Nun," sagte Kaninchen und strich sich über die
Schnurrhaare.

124.2 **"Now you're asking me."**
"Jetzt fragst du mich schon."

125.1 **"I did know once, only I've sort of forgotten,"**
"Ich habe es einmal gewusst, aber ich habe es irgendwie
vergessen,"

125.2 **said Christopher Robin carelessly.**
sagte Christopher Robin achtlos.

126.1 **"It's a funny thing," said Rabbit,**
"Es ist schon komisch," sagte Rabbit,

126.2 **"but I've sort of forgotten too,**
"aber ich habe es auch irgendwie vergessen,

126.3 **although I did know once."**
obwohl ich es einmal wusste."

"I suppose it's just a pole stuck in the ground?"   127.1
"Ich nehme an, es ist nur ein Pfahl, der in der Erde steckt?"

"Sure to be a pole," said Rabbit,   128.1
"Sicherlich ist es ein Pfahl," sagte Rabbit,

"because of calling it a pole, and if it's a pole, well,   128.2
I should think it would be sticking in the ground,
shouldn't you, because there'd be nowhere else to
stick it."
"weil es ein Pfahl ist, und wenn es ein Pfahl ist, dann sollte
man meinen, dass er in der Erde steckt, nicht wahr, weil
man ihn nirgendwo anders hinstecken kann."

"Yes, that's what I thought."   129.1
"Ja, das habe ich mir gedacht."

"The only thing," said Rabbit, "is, where is it   130.1
sticking?"
"Das Einzige," sagte Kaninchen, "ist, wo es hängen bleibt?"

"That's what we're looking for," said Christopher   131.1
Robin.
"Das ist es, was wir suchen," sagte Christopher Robin.

They went back to the others.   132.1
Sie gingen zurück zu den anderen.

Piglet was lying on his back, sleeping peacefully.   132.2
Ferkel lag auf seinem Rücken und schlief friedlich.

132.3 Roo was washing his face and paws in the stream,
while Kanga explained to everybody proudly that
this was the first time he had ever washed his face
himself, and Owl was telling Kanga an Interesting
Anecdote full of long words like Encyclopædia and
Rhododendron to which Kanga wasn't listening.

Ruh wusch sein Gesicht und seine Pfoten im Bach,
während Kanga allen stolz erklärte, dass er sich zum ersten
Mal selbst das Gesicht gewaschen hatte, und Eule erzählte
Kanga eine interessante Anekdote voller langer Wörter
wie Enzyklopädie und Rhododendron, denen Kanga nicht
zuhörte.

133.1 "I don't hold with all this washing,"

"Ich halte nichts von dieser ganzen Wascherei,"

133.2 grumbled Eeyore.

brummte Öhrchen.

133.3 "This modern Behind-the-ears nonsense. What do
you think,

"Dieser moderne Hinter-den-Ohren-Quatsch. Was
denkst du,

133.4 Pooh?"

Puuh?"

134.1 "Well," said Pooh, "I think —— "

"Nun," sagte Puuh, "ich glaube ..."

135.1 But we shall never know what Pooh thought, for
there came a sudden squeak from Roo, a splash, and a
loud cry of alarm from Kanga.

Aber wir werden nie erfahren, was Puuh dachte, denn
plötzlich gab es ein Quietschen von Ruh, ein Platschen und
einen lauten Alarmschrei von Kanga.

"So much for washing," said Eeyore. 136.1

"So viel zum Thema Waschen," sagte I-Aah.

"Roo's fallen in!" cried Rabbit, 137.1

"Ruh ist hineingefallen!" rief Rabbit,

and he and Christopher Robin came rushing down to 137.2
the rescue.

und er und Christopher Robin eilten zur Rettung herbei.

"Look at me swimming!" 139.1

"Sieh mal, wie ich schwimme!"

squeaked Roo from the middle of his pool, and was 139.2
hurried down a waterfall into the next pool.

quietschte Ruh aus der Mitte seines Beckens und wurde
einen Wasserfall hinunter in das nächste Becken
geschleudert.

"Are you all right, Roo dear?" called Kanga anxiously. 140.1

"Geht es dir gut, Roo?" rief Kanga besorgt.

"Yes!" said Roo. "Look at me sw —— " 141.1

"Ja!" sagte Ruh. "Schau, wie ich schw ...,"

238

141.2 and down he went over the next waterfall into
another pool.

und er stürzte über den nächsten Wasserfall in ein anderes
Becken.

142.1 Everybody was doing something to help.

Alle taten etwas, um zu helfen.

142.2 Piglet, wide awake suddenly, was jumping up and
down and making

Ferkel, das plötzlich hellwach war, sprang auf und ab und
machte

142.3 "Oo, I say" noises;

"Oo, sage ich" Geräusche;

142.4 Owl was explaining that in a case of Sudden and
Temporary Immersion the Important Thing was to
keep the Head Above Water;

Eule erklärte, dass es bei plötzlichem und
vorübergehendem Untertauchen wichtig sei, den Kopf
über Wasser zu halten;

142.5 Kanga was jumping along the bank, saying

Kanga sprang am Ufer entlang und sagte

142.6 "Are you sure you're all right, Roo dear?"

"Bist du sicher, dass es dir gut geht, mein lieber Ruh?"

142.7 to which Roo, from whatever pool he was in at the
moment, was answering

worauf Ruh, egal in welchem Becken er sich gerade befand,
antwortete

142.8 "Look at me swimming!"

"Schau, wie ich schwimme!"

Eeyore had turned round and hung his tail over the
first pool into which Roo fell, and with his back to
the accident was grumbling quietly to himself, and
saying,

142.9

I-Aah hatte sich umgedreht und seinen Schwanz über das
erste Becken gehängt, in das Ruh gefallen war, und murrte
mit dem Rücken zu dem Unfall leise vor sich hin und sagte,

"All this washing; but catch on to my tail, little Roo,
and you'll be all right"; and, Christopher Robin and
Rabbit came hurrying past Eeyore, and were calling
out to the others in front of them.

142.10

"So viel Wäsche, aber halt dich an meinem Schwanz fest,
kleiner Ruh, und alles wird gut"; und Christopher Robin
und Kaninchen eilten an I-Aah vorbei und riefen den
anderen vor ihnen etwas zu.

"All right, Roo, I'm coming," called Christopher
Robin.

143.1

"In Ordnung, Ruh, ich komme," rief Christopher Robin.

"Get something across the stream lower down, some
of you fellows,"

144.1

"Holt etwas über den Bach, ein paar von euch,"

called Rabbit.

144.2

rief Rabbit.

But Pooh was getting something.

145.1

Aber Puuh bekam etwas.

145.2 Two pools below Roo he was standing with a long
pole in his paws, and Kanga came up and took one
end of it, and between them they held it across the
lower part of the pool;

Zwei Becken unterhalb von Puuh stand er mit einer langen
Stange in seinen Pfoten, und Kanga kam heran und nahm
ein Ende davon, und sie hielten es über den unteren Teil
des Beckens;

145.3 and Roo, still bubbling proudly,

und Puuh, der immer noch stolz blubberte,

145.4 "Look at me swimming," drifted up against it, and
climbed out.

"Seht mich schwimmen," trieb dagegen und kletterte
heraus.

147.1 "Did you see me swimming?" squeaked Roo excitedly,

"Hast du mich schwimmen sehen?" quietschte Ruh
aufgeregt,

147.2 while Kanga scolded him and rubbed him down.
"Pooh,

während Kanga mit ihm schimpfte und ihn abtrocknete.
"Puuh,

did you see me swimming? That's called swimming, 147.3
hast du mich schwimmen sehen? Das nennt man
schwimmen,

what I was doing. 147.4
was ich da gemacht habe.

Rabbit, did you see what I was doing? Swimming. 147.5
Kaninchen, hast du gesehen, was ich gemacht habe?
Schwimmen.

Hallo, Piglet! I say, Piglet! What do you think I was 147.6
doing! Swimming! Christopher Robin, did you see
me —— "
Hallo, Ferkel! Ich sage, Ferkel! Was glaubst du denn, was
ich da gemacht habe? Schwimmen! Christopher Robin,
hast du mich gesehen ..."

But Christopher Robin wasn't listening. He was 148.1
looking at Pooh.
Aber Christopher Robin hat nicht zugehört. Er schaute
Puuh an.

"Pooh," he said, "where did you find that pole?" 149.1
"Puh," sagte er, "wo hast du diese Stange gefunden?"

Pooh looked at the pole in his hands. 150.1
Puuh betrachtete die Stange in seinen Händen.

"I just found it," he said. 151.1
"Ich habe es gerade gefunden," sagte er.

"I thought it ought to be useful. 151.2
"Ich dachte, es könnte nützlich sein.

242

151.3 I just picked it up."

Ich habe es einfach mitgenommen."

152.1 "Pooh," said Christopher Robin solemnly,

"Puuh," sagte Christopher Robin feierlich,

152.2 "the Expedition is over. You have found the North
Pole!"

"die Expedition ist vorbei. Du hast den Nordpol gefunden!"

153.1 "Oh!" said Pooh.

"Oh!" sagte Puuh.

154.1 Eeyore was sitting with his tail in the water when
they all got back to him.

I-Aah saß mit seinem Schwanz im Wasser, als sie alle zu
ihm zurückkamen.

156.1 "Tell Roo to be quick, somebody," he said.

"Sag Roo, er soll sich beeilen," sagte er.

"My tail's getting cold. I don't want to mention it, 156.2
"Mein Schwanz wird kalt. Ich will es nicht erwähnen,

but I just mention it. 156.3
aber ich erwähne es einfach.

I don't want to complain but there it is. 156.4
Ich will mich nicht beschweren, aber es ist so.

My tail's cold." 156.5
Mein Schwanz ist kalt."

"Here I am!" squeaked Roo. 157.1
"Hier bin ich!" quiekte Ruh.

"Oh, there you are." 158.1
"Oh, da bist du ja."

"Did you see me swimming?" 159.1
"Hast du mich schwimmen sehen?"

Eeyore took his tail out of the water, and swished it 160.1
from side to side.
I-Aah nahm seinen Schwanz aus dem Wasser und
schwenkte ihn hin und her.

"As I expected," he said. "Lost all feeling. 161.1
"Wie ich erwartet habe," sagte er. "Alles Gefühl verloren.

Numbed it. That's what it's done. Numbed it. 161.2
Es betäubt. Das ist es, was es getan hat. Es betäubt.

Well, as long as nobody minds, I suppose it's all 161.3
right."
Nun, solange es niemanden stört, ist es wohl in Ordnung."

244

162.1 "Poor old Eeyore. I'll dry it for you,"
"Armer alter I-Aah. Ich trockne ihn für dich ab,"

162.2 said Christopher Robin,
sagte Christopher Robin,

162.3 and he took out his handkerchief and rubbed it up.
nahm sein Taschentuch heraus und rubbelte ihn ab.

163.1 "Thank you, Christopher Robin.
"Danke, Christopher Robin.

163.2 You're the only one who seems to understand about
tails.
Du bist der Einzige, der etwas von Schwänzen zu verstehen
scheint.

163.3 They don't think -
Sie denken nicht -

163.4 that's what the matter with some of these others.
das ist es, was mit einigen dieser anderen los ist.

163.5 They've no imagination. A tail isn't a tail to them,
Sie haben keine Fantasie. Für sie ist ein Schwanz kein
Schwanz,

163.6 it's just a Little Bit Extra at the back."
sondern nur ein kleines Extra am Hinterteil."

164.1 "Never mind, Eeyore,"
"Schon gut, I- Aah,"

164.2 said Christopher Robin, rubbing his hardest.
sagte Christopher Robin und rieb sich die Hände.

"Is that better?" 164.3
"Ist das besser?"

"It's feeling more like a tail perhaps. 165.1
"Es fühlt sich vielleicht eher wie ein Schwanz an.

It Belongs again, if you know what I mean." 165.2
Es gehört wieder dazu, wenn du weißt, was ich meine."

"Hullo, Eeyore," 166.1
"Hallo, I- Aah,"

said Pooh, coming up to them with his pole. 166.2
sagte Puuh und kam mit seinem Stock auf sie zu.

"Hullo, Pooh. Thank you for asking, 167.1
"Hallo, Puuh. Danke der Nachfrage,

but I shall be able to use it again in a day or two." 167.2
aber ich werde ihn in ein oder zwei Tagen wieder benutzen
können."

"Use what?" said Pooh. 168.1
"Was benutzen?" fragte Puuh.

"What we are talking about." 169.1
"Worüber wir reden."

"I wasn't talking about anything," said Pooh, looking 170.1
puzzled.
"Ich habe von nichts geredet," sagte Pooh und schaute
verwirrt.

171.1 "My mistake again.
"Mein Fehler, schon wieder.

171.2 I thought you were saying how sorry you were about
my tail, being all numb, and could you do anything to
help?"
Ich dachte, Sie sagten, es täte Ihnen leid, dass mein
Schwanz ganz taub ist, und könnten Sie etwas tun, um
zu helfen?"

172.1 "No," said Pooh. "That wasn't me," he said.
"Nein," sagte Puuh. "Das war nicht ich," sagte er.

172.2 He thought for a little and then suggested helpfully,
Er dachte eine Weile nach und schlug dann hilfsbereit vor,

172.3 "Perhaps it was somebody else."
"Vielleicht war es jemand anderes."

173.1 "Well, thank him for me when you see him."
"Nun, danken Sie ihm von mir, wenn Sie ihn sehen."

174.1 Pooh looked anxiously at Christopher Robin.
Puuh schaute Christopher Robin ängstlich an.

175.1 "Pooh's found the North Pole," said Christopher
Robin.
"Puuh hat den Nordpol gefunden," sagte Christopher
Robin.

175.2 "Isn't that lovely?"
"Ist das nicht schön?"

176.1 Pooh looked modestly down.
Puuh schaute bescheiden zu Boden.

"Is that it?" said Eeyore.   177.1
"Ist das alles?" fragte I-Aah.

"Yes," said Christopher Robin.   178.1
"Ja," sagte Christopher Robin.

"Is that what we were looking for?"   179.1
"Ist es das, wonach wir gesucht haben?"

"Yes," said Pooh.   180.1
"Ja," sagte Pooh.

"Oh!" said Eeyore.   181.1
"Oh!" sagte I-Aah.

"Well, anyhow — it didn't rain," he said.   181.2
"Na ja, jedenfalls hat es nicht geregnet," sagte er.

They stuck the pole in the ground,   182.1
Sie steckten den Pfahl in den Boden,

and Christopher Robin tied a message on to it.   182.2
und Christopher Robin band eine Nachricht daran.

NORTH POLE   183.1
NORDPOLEN

DISCOVERED BY POOH   184.1
ENTDECKT VON POOH

POOH FOUND IT.   185.1
POOH HAT ES GEFUNDEN.

187.1 **Then they all went home again.**

Dann gingen sie alle wieder nach Hause.

187.2 **And I think, but I am not quite sure, that Roo had a hot bath and went straight to bed.**

Und ich glaube, aber ich bin mir nicht ganz sicher, dass Ruh ein heißes Bad nahm und direkt ins Bett ging.

187.3 **But Pooh went back to his own house, and feeling very proud of what he had done, had a little something to revive himself.**

Puuh aber ging zurück in sein eigenes Haus und war sehr stolz auf das, was er getan hatte, und nahm eine Kleinigkeit zu sich, um sich zu stärken.

CHAPTER IX · IN WHICH PIGLET IS ENTIRELY SURROUNDED BY WATER

KAPITEL IX · BEI DEM DAS FERKEL VOLLSTÄNDIG VON WASSER UMGEBEN IST

1.1 It rained and it rained and it rained.
Es regnete und regnete und regnete.

1.2 Piglet told himself that never in all his life, and he was goodness knows how old -
Ferkel sagte sich, dass er in seinem ganzen Leben, und er war weiß Gott wie alt -

1.3 three, was it, or four? - never had he seen so much rain.
drei oder vier? - noch nie so viel Regen gesehen hatte.

1.4 Days and days and days.
Tage und Tage und Tage.

2.1 "If only," he thought, as he looked out of the window,
"Wenn ich nur," dachte er, während er aus dem Fenster schaute,

"I had been in Pooh's house, or Christopher Robin's
house, or Rabbit's house when it began to rain, then
I should have had Company all this time, instead
of being here all alone, with nothing to do except
wonder when it will stop."

2.2

"in Puuhs Haus oder in Christopher Robins Haus oder in
Rabbits Haus gewesen wäre, als es zu regnen begann, dann
hätte ich die ganze Zeit über Gesellschaft gehabt, statt hier
ganz allein zu sein und nichts zu tun, außer mich zu fragen,
wann es aufhören wird."

And he imagined himself with Pooh, saying,

2.3

Und er stellte sich vor, wie er zu Puuh sagte,

"Did you ever see such rain, Pooh?" and Pooh saying,

2.4

"Hast du jemals so einen Regen gesehen, Puuh?" und Puuh
sagte,

"Isn't it awful, Piglet?" and Piglet saying,

2.5

"Ist es nicht schrecklich, Ferkel?" und Ferkel sagte,

"I wonder how it is over Christopher Robin's way"

2.6

"Ich frage mich, wie es drüben bei Christopher Robin
aussieht,"

and Pooh saying,

2.7

und Puuh sagte,

"I should think poor old Rabbit is about flooded out
by this time."

2.8

"Ich glaube, der arme alte Rabbit ist inzwischen
überschwemmt."

2.9 It would have been jolly to talk like this, and really, it wasn't much good having anything exciting like floods, if you couldn't share them with somebody.

Es wäre lustig gewesen, sich so zu unterhalten, und es war wirklich nicht gut, so etwas Aufregendes wie Überschwemmungen zu haben, wenn man sie nicht mit jemandem teilen konnte.

3.1 For it was rather exciting.

Denn es war ziemlich aufregend.

3.2 The little dry ditches in which Piglet had nosed about so often had become streams, the little streams across which he had splashed were rivers, and the river, between whose steep banks they had played so happily, had sprawled out of its own bed and was taking up so much room everywhere, that Piglet was beginning to wonder whether it would be coming into his bed soon.

Die kleinen trockenen Gräben, in denen Ferkel so oft herumgeschnüffelt hatte, waren zu Bächen geworden, die kleinen Bäche, durch die er geplätschert war, zu Flüssen, und der Fluss, zwischen dessen steilen Ufern sie so vergnügt gespielt hatten, hatte sich aus seinem eigenen Bett ausgebreitet und nahm überall so viel Platz ein, dass Ferkel sich zu fragen begann, ob er bald in sein Bett kommen würde.

4.1 "It's a little Anxious," he said to himself,

"Es ist ein wenig beängstigend," sagte er zu sich selbst,

4.2 "to be a Very Small Animal Entirely Surrounded by Water.

"ein sehr kleines Tier zu sein, das vollständig von Wasser umgeben ist.

Christopher Robin and Pooh could escape by 4.3
Climbing Trees, and Kanga could escape by Jumping,
and Rabbit could escape by Burrowing, and Owl
could escape by Flying, and Eeyore could escape by —
by Making a Loud Noise Until Rescued, and here am I,
surrounded by water and I can't do anything."

Christopher Robin und Pooh konnten entkommen, indem
sie auf Bäume kletterten, und Kanga konnte entkommen,
indem er sprang, und Kaninchen konnte entkommen,
indem es grub, und Eule konnte entkommen, indem sie
flog, und I — Aah konnte entkommen, indem er ein lautes
Geräusch machte, bis er gerettet wurde, und hier bin ich,
umgeben von Wasser und ich kann nichts tun."

It went on raining, and every day the water got a 5.1
little higher, until now it was nearly up to Piglet's
window ...

Es regnete weiter, und jeden Tag stieg das Wasser ein
wenig höher, bis es schließlich fast bis zu Ferkels Fenster
reichte ...

and still he hadn't done anything. 5.2

und er hatte immer noch nichts getan.

7.1 "There's Pooh," he thought to himself.
"Da ist Pooh," dachte er bei sich.

7.2 "Pooh hasn't much Brain, but he never comes to any
harm.
"Pooh hat nicht viel Hirn, aber er kommt nie zu Schaden.

7.3 He does silly things and they turn out right.
Er macht dumme Sachen, und sie gehen gut aus.

7.4 There's Owl. Owl hasn't exactly got Brain,
Dann ist da noch Eule. Eule hat nicht gerade ein Gehirn,

7.5 but he Knows Things.
aber er weiß Dinge.

7.6 He would know the Right Thing to Do when
Surrounded by Water.
Er würde wissen, was zu tun ist, wenn er von Wasser
umgeben ist.

7.7 There's Rabbit. He hasn't Learnt in Books,
Da ist der Hase. Er hat nicht in Büchern gelernt,

7.8 but he can always Think of a Clever Plan.
aber er kann sich immer einen schlauen Plan ausdenken.

7.9 There's Kanga.
Da ist Kanga.

7.10 She isn't Clever, Kanga isn't, but she would be so
anxious about Roo that she would do a Good Thing to
Do without thinking about It.
Kanga ist nicht schlau, aber sie würde sich so sehr um Ruh
sorgen, dass sie eine gute Sache tun würde, ohne darüber
nachzudenken.

And then there's Eeyore. 7.11

Und dann ist da noch Eeyore.

And Eeyore is so miserable anyhow that he wouldn't 7.12
mind about this.

Und I-Aah ist sowieso so unglücklich, dass ihm das nichts
ausmachen würde.

But I wonder what Christopher Robin would do?" 7.13

Aber ich frage mich, was Christopher Robin tun würde?"

Then suddenly he remembered a story which 8.1
Christopher Robin had told him about a man on a
desert island who had written something in a bottle
and thrown it in the sea;

Plötzlich erinnerte er sich an eine Geschichte, die
Christopher Robin ihm erzählt hatte, von einem Mann auf
einer einsamen Insel, der etwas in eine Flasche geschrieben
und sie ins Meer geworfen hatte;

and Piglet thought that if he wrote something in a 8.2
bottle and threw it in the water, perhaps somebody
would come and rescue him!

und Ferkel dachte, wenn er etwas in eine Flasche schrieb
und sie ins Wasser warf, würde vielleicht jemand kommen
und ihn retten!

He left the window and began to search his house, 9.1
all of it that wasn't under water, and at last he found
a pencil and a small piece of dry paper, and a bottle
with a cork to it.

Er verließ das Fenster und begann, sein Haus zu
durchsuchen, alles, was nicht unter Wasser stand, und
schließlich fand er einen Bleistift und ein kleines Stück
trockenes Papier und eine Flasche mit einem Korken
darauf.

9.2 And he wrote on one side of the paper:
Und er schrieb auf eine Seite des Papiers:

HELP!   HILFE!

PIGLET (ME)   PIGLET (ME)

11.1 and on the other side:
und auf der anderen Seite:

12.1 IT'S ME PIGLET, HELP HELP.
ICH BIN'S, FERKEL, HILFE, HILFE.

13.1 Then he put the paper in the bottle, and he corked the
bottle up as tightly as he could, and he leant out of his
window as far as he could lean without falling in, and
he threw the bottle as far as he could throw — splash!
Dann steckte er das Papier in die Flasche, verschloss sie so
fest wie möglich, lehnte sich so weit wie möglich aus dem
Fenster, ohne hineinzufallen, und warf die Flasche so weit,
wie er sie werfen konnte — platsch!

13.2 — and in a little while it bobbed up again on the
water;
— und nach kurzer Zeit trieb sie wieder auf dem Wasser;

and he watched it floating slowly away in the 13.3
distance, until his eyes ached with looking, and
sometimes he thought it was the bottle, and
sometimes he thought it was just a ripple on the
water which he was following, and then suddenly he
knew that he would never see it again and that he had
done all that he could do to save himself.

und er sah zu, wie sie langsam in die Ferne trieb, bis ihm
die Augen vom Hinsehen weh taten, und manchmal dachte
er, es sei die Flasche, und manchmal dachte er, es sei nur
ein Plätschern auf dem Wasser, dem er folgte, und dann
wusste er plötzlich, dass er sie nie wieder sehen würde und
dass er alles getan hatte, was er tun konnte, um sich zu
retten.

"So now," he thought, 15.1

"Jetzt," dachte er,

"somebody else will have to do something, and I hope 15.2
they will do it soon, because if they don't I shall have
to swim, which I can't, so I hope they do it soon."

"muss jemand anders etwas tun, und ich hoffe, dass er es
bald tut, denn sonst muss ich schwimmen, was ich nicht
kann, also hoffe ich, dass er es bald tut."

And then he gave a very long sigh and said, 15.3

Dann stieß er einen langen Seufzer aus und sagte,

15.4 "I wish Pooh were here.

"Ich wünschte, Pooh wäre hier.

15.5 It's so much more friendly with two."

Es ist so viel freundlicher zu zweit."

17.1 When the rain began Pooh was asleep.

Als der Regen begann, schlief Puuh.

17.2 It rained, and it rained, and it rained, and he slept
and he slept and he slept.

Es regnete und regnete und regnete, und er schlief und
schlief und schlief.

17.3 He had had a tiring day.

Er hatte einen anstrengenden Tag hinter sich.

17.4 You remember how he discovered the North Pole;

Du erinnerst dich, wie er den Nordpol entdeckte;

17.5 well, he was so proud of this that he asked
Christopher Robin if there were any other Poles such
as a Bear of Little Brain might discover.

nun, er war so stolz darauf, dass er Christopher Robin
fragte, ob es noch andere Pole gäbe, die ein Bär von Little
Brain entdecken könnte.

18.1 "There's a South Pole," said Christopher Robin,

"Es gibt einen Südpol," sagte Christopher Robin,

"and I expect there's an East Pole and a West Pole, 18.2
though people don't like talking about them."

"und ich nehme an, es gibt auch einen Ost - und einen
Westpol, auch wenn die Leute nicht gerne darüber
sprechen."

Pooh was very excited when he heard this, and 19.1
suggested that they should have an Expotition to
discover the East Pole, but Christopher Robin had
thought of something else to do with Kanga; so Pooh
went out to discover the East Pole by himself.

Puuh war sehr aufgeregt, als er das hörte, und schlug
vor, eine Expedition zur Entdeckung des Ostpols zu
veranstalten, aber Christopher Robin hatte sich etwas
anderes ausgedacht, was er mit Kanga machen konnte, und
so ging Puuh los, um den Ostpol selbst zu entdecken.

Whether he discovered it or not, I forget; but he was 19.2
so tired when he got home that, in the very middle
of his supper, after he had been eating for little more
than half-an-hour, he fell fast asleep in his chair, and
slept and slept and slept.

Ob er ihn entdeckt hat oder nicht, weiß ich nicht mehr,
aber er war so müde, als er nach Hause kam, dass er mitten
beim Abendessen, nachdem er kaum mehr als eine halbe
Stunde gegessen hatte, in seinem Stuhl fest einschlief und
schlief und schlief und schlief.

Then suddenly he was dreaming. He was at the East 20.1
Pole,

Dann träumte er plötzlich. Er befand sich am Ostpol,

and it was a very cold pole with the coldest sort of 20.2
snow and ice all over it.

und es war ein sehr kalter Pol mit der kältesten Art von
Schnee und Eis überall auf ihm.

20.3 He had found a bee-hive to sleep in, but there wasn't
room for his legs, so he had left them outside.

Er hatte einen Bienenstock gefunden, in dem er schlafen
konnte, aber es gab keinen Platz für seine Beine, also hatte
er sie draußen gelassen.

20.4 And Wild Woozles, such as inhabit the East Pole,
came and nibbled all the fur off his legs to make nests
for their Young.

Und die wilden Wölflinge, die am Ostpol leben, kamen und
knabberten ihm das ganze Fell von den Beinen, um Nester
für ihre Jungen zu bauen.

20.5 And the more they nibbled, the colder his legs got,
until suddenly he woke up with an Ow! -

Und je mehr sie knabberten, desto kälter wurden seine
Beine, bis er plötzlich mit einem "Aua" aufwachte -

20.6 and there he was, sitting in his chair with his feet in
the water, and water all round him!

und da saß er nun in seinem Stuhl, mit den Füßen im
Wasser, und überall war Wasser um ihn herum!

21.1 He splashed to his door and looked out ...

Er plätscherte zu seiner Tür und schaute hinaus ...

22.1 "This is Serious," said Pooh.

"Das ist eine ernste Sache," sagte Pooh.

22.2 "I must have an Escape."

"Ich brauche einen Ausweg."

So he took his largest pot of honey and escaped with
it to a broad branch of his tree, well above the water,
and then he climbed down again and escaped with
another pot ...

23.1

Also nahm er seinen größten Honigtopf und flüchtete
damit auf einen breiten Ast seines Baumes, weit über
dem Wasser, und dann kletterte er wieder hinunter und
flüchtete mit einem anderen Topf ...

and when the whole Escape was finished, there was
Pooh sitting on his branch, dangling his legs, and
there, beside him, were ten pots of honey ...

23.2

und als die ganze Flucht beendet war, saß Puuh auf seinem
Ast und ließ die Beine baumeln, und neben ihm standen
zehn Honigtöpfe ...

Two days later, there was Pooh, sitting on his branch,
dangling his legs, and there, beside him, were four
pots of honey ...

25.1

Zwei Tage später saß Puuh auf seinem Ast und ließ die
Beine baumeln, und neben ihm standen vier Töpfe mit
Honig ...

26.1 Three days later, there was Pooh, sitting on his
branch, dangling his legs, and there beside him,
was one pot of honey.

Drei Tage später saß Puuh auf seinem Ast und ließ die
Beine baumeln, und neben ihm stand ein Topf mit Honig.

27.1 Four days later, there was Pooh ...

Vier Tage später war Pooh da ...

29.1 And it was on the morning of the fourth day that
Piglet's bottle came floating past him, and with one
loud cry of

Und es war am Morgen des vierten Tages, als Ferkels
Flasche an ihm vorbeischwamm, und mit einem lauten
Schrei

29.2 "Honey!"

"Schatz!"

29.3 Pooh plunged into the water, seized the bottle, and
struggled back to his tree again.

stürzte sich Puuh ins Wasser, ergriff die Flasche und
kämpfte sich wieder zu seinem Baum zurück.

"Bother!" said Pooh, as he opened it.   30.1
"Mist!" sagte Puuh, als er ihn öffnete.

"All that wet for nothing. What's that bit of paper   30.2
doing?"
"All das Nass für nichts. Was soll das Stück Papier?"

He took it out and looked at it.   31.1
Er nahm sie heraus und betrachtete sie.

"It's a Missage," he said to himself,   32.1
"Es ist eine Missage," sagte er zu sich selbst,

"that's what it is. And that letter is a 'P,'   32.2
"das ist es. Und dieser Buchstabe ist ein 'P,'

and so is that, and so is that, and 'P' means 'Pooh,'   32.3
und so ist das, und so ist das, und 'P' bedeutet 'Pooh,'

so it's a very important Missage to me,   32.4
also ist es ein sehr wichtiger Missage für mich,

and I can't read it.   32.5
und ich kann ihn nicht lesen.

I must find Christopher Robin or Owl or Piglet, one of   32.6
those Clever Readers who can read things, and they
will tell me what this missage means.
Ich muss Christopher Robin oder Eule oder Ferkel finden,
einen von diesen schlauen Lesern, die Dinge lesen können,
und sie werden mir sagen, was diese Missage bedeutet.

Only I can't swim. Bother!"   32.7
Aber ich kann nicht schwimmen. So ein Mist!"

33.1 Then he had an idea, and I think that for a Bear of
Very Little Brain, it was a good idea.

Dann hatte er eine Idee, und ich glaube, für einen Bären
mit sehr wenig Hirn war das eine gute Idee.

33.2 He said to himself:

Er sagte zu sich selbst:

34.1 "If a bottle can float, then a jar can float, and if a jar
floats, I can sit on the top of it, if it's a very big jar."

"Wenn eine Flasche schwimmen kann, dann kann auch ein
Glas schwimmen, und wenn ein Glas schwimmt, kann ich
mich oben drauf setzen, wenn es ein sehr großes Glas ist."

36.1 So he took his biggest jar, and corked it up.

Also nahm er sein größtes Glas und verschloss es mit einem
Korken.

36.2 "All boats have to have a name," he said,

"Alle Boote müssen einen Namen haben," sagte er,

36.3 "so I shall call mine The Floating Bear."

"also werde ich meins Der schwimmende Bär nennen."

And with these words he dropped his boat into the   36.4
water and jumped in after it.

Und mit diesen Worten ließ er sein Boot ins Wasser fallen
und sprang hinterher.

For a little while Pooh and The Floating Bear were   38.1
uncertain as to which of them was meant to be
on the top, but after trying one or two different
positions, they settled down with The Floating
Bear underneath and Pooh triumphantly astride it,
paddling vigorously with his feet.

Eine Weile waren Puuh und der schwimmende Bär
unsicher, wer von ihnen oben sein sollte, aber nachdem
sie ein oder zwei verschiedene Positionen ausprobiert
hatten, ließen sie sich nieder, wobei der schwimmende Bär
unten war und Puuh triumphierend rittlings darauf saß
und kräftig mit seinen Füßen paddelte.

40.1 Christopher Robin lived at the very top of the Forest.

Christopher Robin wohnte ganz oben im Wald.

40.2 It rained, and it rained, and it rained, but the water couldn't come up to his house.

Es regnete und regnete und regnete, aber das Wasser konnte nicht bis zu seinem Haus kommen.

40.3 It was rather jolly to look down into the valleys and see the water all round him, but it rained so hard that he stayed indoors most of the time, and thought about things.

Es war ziemlich lustig, in die Täler hinunterzuschauen und das Wasser um ihn herum zu sehen, aber es regnete so stark, dass er die meiste Zeit im Haus blieb und über Dinge nachdachte.

40.4 Every morning he went out with his umbrella and put a stick in the place where the water came up to, and every next morning he went out and couldn't see his stick any more, so he put another stick in the place where the water came up to, and then he walked home again, and each morning he had a shorter way to walk than he had had the morning before.

Jeden Morgen ging er mit seinem Regenschirm hinaus und steckte einen Stock in die Stelle, an der das Wasser hochkam, und jeden nächsten Morgen ging er hinaus und konnte seinen Stock nicht mehr sehen, also steckte er einen anderen Stock in die Stelle, an der das Wasser hochkam, und dann ging er wieder nach Hause, und jeden Morgen hatte er einen kürzeren Weg zu gehen als am Morgen zuvor.

On the morning of the fifth day he saw the water all round him, and knew that for the first time in his life he was on a real island.

40.5

Am Morgen des fünften Tages sah er das Wasser um sich herum, und er wusste, dass er zum ersten Mal in seinem Leben auf einer richtigen Insel war.

Which was very exciting.

40.6

Das war sehr aufregend.

It was on this morning that Owl came flying over the water to say

42.1

An diesem Morgen kam die Eule über das Wasser geflogen

"How do you do," to his friend Christopher Robin.

42.2

"Guten Tag," um seinem Freund Christopher Robin zu sagen.

"I say, Owl," said Christopher Robin,

43.1

"Sag mal, Eule," sagte Christopher Robin,

43.2 "isn't this fun? I'm on an island!"
"ist das nicht lustig? Ich bin auf einer Insel!"

44.1 "The atmospheric conditions have been very
unfavourable lately,"
"Die atmosphärischen Bedingungen waren in letzter Zeit
sehr ungünstig,"

44.2 said Owl.
sagte Eule.

45.1 "The what?"
"Die was?"

46.1 "It has been raining," explained Owl.
"Es hat geregnet," erklärte Eule.

47.1 "Yes," said Christopher Robin. "It has."
"Ja," sagte Christopher Robin. "Das hat es."

48.1 "The flood-level has reached an unprecedented
height."
"Der Hochwasserpegel hat eine noch nie dagewesene Höhe
erreicht."

49.1 "The who?"
"Der wer?"

50.1 "There's a lot of water about," explained Owl.
"Hier gibt es viel Wasser," erklärte Eule.

51.1 "Yes," said Christopher Robin, "there is."
"Ja," sagte Christopher Robin, "die gibt es."

"However, the prospects are rapidly becoming more
favourable.

"Die Aussichten werden jedoch schnell günstiger.

52.1

At any moment —— "

Jeden Moment ..."

52.2

"Have you seen Pooh?"

"Hast du Puuh gesehen?"

53.1

"No. At any moment —— "

"Nein. Jeden Moment ..."

54.1

"I hope he's all right," said Christopher Robin.

"Ich hoffe, es geht ihm gut," sagte Christopher Robin.

55.1

"I've been wondering about him.

"Ich habe mir schon Sorgen um ihn gemacht.

55.2

I expect Piglet's with him.

Ich nehme an, Ferkel ist bei ihm.

55.3

Do you think they're all right, Owl?"

Glaubst du, dass es ihnen gut geht, Eule?"

55.4

"I expect so. You see, at any moment —— "

"Ich erwarte es. Du siehst, jeden Moment ..."

56.1

"Do go and see, Owl.

"Geh und sieh nach, Eule.

57.1

Because Pooh hasn't got very much brain, and he
might do something silly, and I do love him so, Owl.

Denn Puuh hat nicht viel Verstand und könnte etwas
Dummes tun, und ich liebe ihn so sehr, Eule.

57.2

57.3 Do you see, Owl?"

Siehst du, Eule?"

58.1 "That's all right," said Owl. "I'll go.

"Das ist in Ordnung," sagte Eule. "Ich werde gehen.

58.2 Back directly." And he flew off.

Bin gleich zurück." Und er flog los.

59.1 In a little while he was back again.

Nach kurzer Zeit war er wieder da.

60.1 "Pooh isn't there," he said.

"Pooh ist nicht da," sagte er.

61.1 "Not there?"

"Nicht da?"

62.1 "Has been there.

"Er war dort.

62.2 He's been sitting on a branch of his tree outside his house with nine pots of honey.

Er saß auf einem Ast seines Baumes vor seinem Haus mit neun Töpfen Honig.

62.3 But he isn't there now."

Aber jetzt ist er nicht mehr da."

63.1 "Oh, Pooh!" cried Christopher Robin. "Where are you?"

"Oh, Puuh!" rief Christopher Robin. "Wo bist du?"

"Here I am," said a growly voice behind him.   65.1

"Hier bin ich," sagte eine knurrige Stimme hinter ihm.

"Pooh!"   66.1

"Puh!"

They rushed into each other's arms.   67.1

Sie stürzten sich in die Arme des anderen.

"How did you get here, Pooh?" asked Christopher   68.1
Robin,

"Wie bist du hierher gekommen, Puuh?" fragte
Christopher Robin,

when he was ready to talk again.   68.2

als er wieder sprechen konnte.

"On my boat," said Pooh proudly.   69.1

"Auf meinem Boot," sagte Pooh stolz.

69.2 "I had a Very Important Missage sent me in a bottle,
and owing to having got some water in my eyes, I
couldn't read it, so I brought it to you.

"Ich habe eine sehr wichtige Nachricht in einer Flasche
geschickt bekommen, und weil ich etwas Wasser in die
Augen bekommen habe, konnte ich sie nicht lesen, also
habe ich sie dir gebracht.

69.3 On my boat."

Auf meinem Boot."

71.1 With these proud words he gave Christopher Robin
the missage.

Mit diesen stolzen Worten gab er Christopher Robin den
Laufpass.

72.1 "But it's from Piglet!"

"Aber er ist von Ferkel!"

72.2 cried Christopher Robin when he had read it.

rief Christopher Robin, als er ihn gelesen hatte.

73.1 "Isn't there anything about Pooh in it?"

"Steht da nichts über Pooh drin?"

asked Bear, looking over his shoulder.   73.2
fragte Bär und schaute über seine Schulter.

Christopher Robin read the message aloud.   74.1
Christopher Robin las die Nachricht laut vor.

"Oh, are those 'P's' piglets? I thought they were   75.1
poohs."
"Oh, sind das 'P's' Ferkel? Ich dachte, das wären Puhs."

"We must rescue him at once!   76.1
"Wir müssen ihn sofort retten!

I thought he was with you, Pooh. Owl,   76.2
Ich dachte, er wäre bei dir, Puuh. Eule,

could you rescue him on your back?"   76.3
kannst du ihn auf deinem Rücken retten?"

"I don't think so," said Owl, after grave thought.   77.1
"Das glaube ich nicht," sagte Eule nach reiflicher
Überlegung.

"It is doubtful if the necessary dorsal muscles —— "   77.2
"Es ist fraglich, ob die notwendigen Rückenmuskeln ..."

"Then would you fly to him at once and say that   78.1
Rescue is Coming?
"Würdest du dann sofort zu ihm fliegen und ihm sagen,
dass die Rettung naht?

And Pooh and I will think of a Rescue and come as   78.2
quick as ever we can.
Und Puuh und ich werden an eine Rettung denken und so
schnell wie möglich kommen.

78.3 Oh, don't talk, Owl, go on quick!"

Oh, sprich nicht, Eule, flieg schnell!"

78.4 And, still thinking of something to say, Owl flew off.

Und während sie noch überlegte, was sie sagen sollte, flog
Eule los.

79.1 "Now then, Pooh," said Christopher Robin,

"Nun denn, Puuh," sagte Christopher Robin,

79.2 "where's your boat?"

"wo ist dein Boot?"

80.1 "I ought to say,"

"Ich muss sagen,"

80.2 explained Pooh as they walked down to the shore of
the island,

erklärte Pooh, während sie zum Ufer der Insel
hinuntergingen,

80.3 "that it isn't just an ordinary sort of boat.

"dass es sich nicht um ein gewöhnliches Boot handelt.

80.4 Sometimes it's a Boat, and sometimes it's more of an
Accident.

Manchmal ist es ein Boot, und manchmal ist es eher ein
Unfall.

80.5 It all depends."

Das kommt ganz darauf an."

81.1 "Depends on what?"

"Hängt wovon ab?"

"On whether I'm on the top of it or underneath it." 82.1

"Darüber, ob ich oben oder unten bin."

"Oh! Well, where is it?" 83.1

"Oh! Nun, wo ist es?"

"There!" said Pooh, pointing proudly to The Floating 84.1
Bear.

"Da!" sagte Puuh und zeigte stolz auf den Schwebenden
Bären.

It wasn't what Christopher Robin expected, and 85.1
the more he looked at it, the more he thought what
a Brave and Clever Bear Pooh was, and the more
Christopher Robin thought this, the more Pooh
looked modestly down his nose and tried to pretend
he wasn't.

Es war nicht das, was Christopher Robin erwartet hatte,
und je mehr er es ansah, desto mehr dachte er, was für ein
tapferer und kluger Bär Puuh war, und je mehr Christopher
Robin dies dachte, desto bescheidener schaute Puuh in die
Nase und versuchte, so zu tun, als wäre er es nicht.

"But it's too small for two of us," 86.1

"Aber es ist zu klein für uns beide,"

said Christopher Robin sadly. 86.2

sagte Christopher Robin traurig.

"Three of us with Piglet." 87.1

"Drei von uns mit Ferkel."

"That makes it smaller still. 88.1

"Das macht ihn noch kleiner.

88.2 Oh, Pooh Bear, what shall we do?"

Oh, Puuh-Bär, was sollen wir tun?"

89.1 And then this Bear, Pooh Bear, Winnie-the-Pooh,
F.O.P. (Friend of Piglet's), R.C. (Rabbit's Companion),
P.D. (Pole Discoverer), E.C. and T.F. (Eeyore's
Comforter and Tail- finder) -

Und dann sagte dieser Bär, Puuh-Bär, Winnie-the-Pooh,
F.O.P. (Freund von Ferkel), R.C. (Rabbit's Companion), P.D.
(Pole Discoverer), E.C. und T.F. (Eeyore's Comforter and
Tail- finder) -

89.2 in fact, Pooh himself -

ja, Puuh selbst -

89.3 said something so clever that Christopher Robin
could only look at him with mouth open and eyes
staring, wondering if this was really the Bear of Very
Little Brain whom he had known and loved so long.

etwas so Kluges, dass Christopher Robin ihn nur mit
offenem Mund und starrenden Augen ansehen konnte
und sich fragte, ob dies wirklich der Bär von Very Little
Brain war, den er so lange gekannt und geliebt hatte.

90.1 "We might go in your umbrella," said Pooh.

"Wir könnten mit deinem Regenschirm gehen," sagte
Pooh.

91.1 "? "

"? "

92.1 "We might go in your umbrella," said Pooh.

"Wir könnten mit deinem Regenschirm gehen," sagte
Pooh.

"? ? "   93.1
"? ? "

"We might go in your umbrella," said Pooh.   94.1
"Wir könnten mit deinem Regenschirm gehen," sagte
Pooh.

"! ! ! ! ! ! "   95.1
"! ! ! ! ! ! "

For suddenly Christopher Robin saw that they might.   96.1
Denn plötzlich sah Christopher Robin, dass sie es könnten.

He opened his umbrella and put it point downwards   96.2
in the water.
Er öffnete seinen Regenschirm und hielt ihn mit der Spitze
nach unten ins Wasser.

It floated but wobbled. Pooh got in.   96.3
Er schwamm, aber er wackelte. Puuh stieg ein.

He was just beginning to say that it was all right   96.4
now, when he found that it wasn't, so after a short
drink which he didn't really want he waded back to
Christopher Robin.
Er wollte gerade sagen, dass jetzt alles in Ordnung sei, als
er merkte, dass es nicht so war, und nach einem kurzen
Schluck, den er eigentlich nicht wollte, watete er zu
Christopher Robin zurück.

Then they both got in together,   96.5
Dann stiegen sie beide zusammen ein,

and it wobbled no longer.   96.6
und es wackelte nicht mehr.

98.1 "I shall call this boat The Brain of Pooh,"

"Ich werde dieses Boot Das Hirn von Pooh nennen,"

98.2 said Christopher Robin, and The Brain of Pooh set sail forthwith in a south-westerly direction, revolving gracefully.

sagte Christopher Robin, und das Hirn von Pooh setzte sofort die Segel in Richtung Südwesten und drehte sich anmutig.

You can imagine Piglet's joy when at last the ship
came in sight of him.

100.1

Du kannst dir Ferkels Freude vorstellen, als das Schiff
endlich in Sichtweite kam.

100.2 In after-years he liked to think that he had been in Very Great Danger during the Terrible Flood, but the only danger he had really been in was in the last half-hour of his imprisonment, when Owl, who had just flown up, sat on a branch of his tree to comfort him, and told him a very long story about an aunt who had once laid a seagull's egg by mistake, and the story went on and on, rather like this sentence, until Piglet who was listening out of his window without much hope, went to sleep quietly and naturally, slipping slowly out of the window towards the water until he was only hanging on by his toes, at which moment luckily, a sudden loud squawk from Owl, which was really part of the story, being what his aunt said, woke the Piglet up and just gave him time to jerk himself back into safety and say,

In späteren Jahren dachte er gerne, dass er während der schrecklichen Flut in sehr großer Gefahr gewesen war, Aber die einzige Gefahr, der er wirklich ausgesetzt war, war die letzte halbe Stunde seiner Gefangenschaft, als die Eule, die gerade hochgeflogen war, sich auf einen Ast seines Baumes setzte, um ihn zu trösten, und ihm eine lange Geschichte über eine Tante erzählte, die einmal aus Versehen ein Möwenei gelegt hatte, und die Geschichte ging immer weiter, ungefähr wie dieser Satz, bis Ferkel, das ohne große Hoffnung aus dem Fenster lauschte, ganz ruhig und natürlich einschlief, Er rutschte langsam aus dem Fenster Richtung Wasser, bis er sich nur noch an den Zehen festhalten konnte, In diesem Moment ertönte zum Glück plötzlich ein lautes Kreischen von Eule, ein lauter Schrei von Eule, der eigentlich zu der Geschichte gehörte, die seine Tante erzählte, das Ferkel aufweckte und gab ihm gerade noch Zeit, sich mit einem Ruck wieder in Sicherheit zu bringen und zu sagen,

100.3 "How interesting, and did she?" when -

"Wie interessant, und hat sie?" wenn -

well, you can imagine his joy when at last he saw the
good ship, Brain of Pooh (Captain, C. Robin;

100.4

Du kannst dir seine Freude vorstellen, als er endlich das
gute Schiff Brain of Pooh (Kapitän C. Robin;

1st Mate,

100.5

1. Maat P. Bär) über das Meer kommen sah,

P. Bear) coming over the sea to rescue him.

100.6

um ihn zu retten.

Christopher Robin and Pooh again ...

100.7

Christopher Robin und Pooh wieder ...

And that is really the end of the story, and I am very
tired after that last sentence, I think I shall stop
there.

102.1

Und das ist wirklich das Ende der Geschichte, und ich bin
nach diesem letzten Satz sehr müde, ich denke, ich sollte
hier aufhören.

CHAPTER X · IN WHICH CHRISTOPHER ROBIN GIVES POOH A PARTY, AND WE SAY GOOD-BYE

KAPITEL X · IN DEM CHRISTOPHER ROBIN EINE PARTY FÜR POOH GIBT UND WIR UNS VERABSCHIEDEN

One day when the sun had come back over the Forest,   1.1
bringing with it the scent of may, and all the streams
of the Forest were tinkling happily to find themselves
their own pretty shape again, and the little pools lay
dreaming of the life they had seen and the big things
they had done, and in the warmth and quiet of the
Forest the cuckoo was trying over his voice carefully
and listening to see if he liked it, and wood-pigeons
were complaining gently to themselves in their lazy
comfortable way that it was the other fellow's fault,
but it didn't matter very much;

Eines Tages, als die Sonne wieder über den Wald
gekommen war und den Duft des Mai mit sich brachte, und
alle Bäche des Waldes fröhlich plätscherten, um wieder
ihre eigene schöne Form zu finden, und die kleinen Tümpel
lagen und träumten von dem Leben, das sie gesehen
und den großen Dingen, die sie getan hatten, und in der
Wärme und Stille des Waldes probierte der Kuckuck seine
Stimme vorsichtig aus und lauschte, ob sie ihm gefiel, und
die Ringeltauben beschwerten sich leise auf ihre faule,
bequeme Art, dass der andere schuld war, aber das war
nicht so schlimm;

on such a day as this Christopher Robin whistled in   1.2
a special way he had, and Owl came flying out of the
Hundred Acre Wood to see what was wanted.

An einem Tag wie diesem pfiff Christopher Robin auf
eine ganz besondere Weise, und Eule kam aus dem
Hundertmorgenwald geflogen, um zu sehen, was er wollte.

3.1 "Owl," said Christopher Robin,

"Eule," sagte Christopher Robin,

3.2 "I am going to give a party."

"ich werde eine Party geben."

4.1 "You are, are you?" said Owl.

"Du bist es, nicht wahr?" sagte Eule.

5.1 "And it's to be a special sort of party, because it's
because of what Pooh did when he did what he did to
save Piglet from the flood."

"Und es soll eine ganz besondere Party werden, denn es
geht darum, was Puuh getan hat, als er Ferkel vor der Flut
gerettet hat."

6.1 "Oh, that's what it's for, is it?" said Owl.

"Ach, dafür ist es also da?" sagte Eule.

"Yes, so will you tell Pooh as quickly as you can, and all the others, because it will be to- morrow." 7.1

"Ja, sag es Pooh so schnell wie möglich, und allen anderen, denn es wird morgen sein."

"Oh, it will, will it?" said Owl, 8.1

"Oh, das wird es, nicht wahr?" sagte Eule,

still being as helpful as possible. 8.2

immer noch so hilfreich wie möglich.

"So will you go and tell them, Owl?" 9.1

"Wirst du es ihnen also sagen, Eule?"

Owl tried to think of something very wise to say, but couldn't, so he flew off to tell the others. 10.1

Eule versuchte, etwas sehr Kluges zu sagen, konnte es aber nicht, also flog er los, um es den anderen zu sagen.

And the first person he told was Pooh. 10.2

Und die erste Person, der er es erzählte, war Puuh.

"Pooh," he said, "Christopher Robin is giving a party." 11.1

"Puuh," sagte er, "Christopher Robin gibt eine Party."

"Oh!" said Pooh. 12.1

"Oh!" sagte Puuh.

And then seeing that Owl expected him to say something else, he said 12.2

Und als er sah, dass Eule erwartete, dass er etwas anderes sagen würde, sagte er,

12.3 "Will there be those little cake things with pink sugar
icing?"

"Gibt es diese kleinen Kuchendinger mit rosa Zuckerguss?"

13.1 Owl felt that it was rather beneath him to talk about
little cake things with pink sugar icing, so he told
Pooh exactly what Christopher Robin had said, and
flew off to Eeyore.

Eule fand, dass es unter seiner Würde war, über kleine
Törtchen mit rosa Zuckerguss zu reden, also sagte er Puuh
genau das, was Christopher Robin gesagt hatte, und flog zu
I-Aah.

15.1 "A party for Me?" thought Pooh to himself.

"Eine Party für mich?" dachte Puuh bei sich.

15.2 "How grand!"

"Wie großartig!"

And he began to wonder if all the other animals would know that it was a special Pooh Party, and if Christopher Robin had told them about The Floating Bear and the Brain of Pooh and all the wonderful ships he had invented and sailed on, and he began to think how awful it would be if everybody had forgotten about it, and nobody quite knew what the party was for; 15.3

Und er begann sich zu fragen, ob all die anderen Tiere wissen würden, dass es eine besondere Puuh-Party war, und ob Christopher Robin ihnen von dem schwimmenden Bären und dem Gehirn von Puuh und all den wunderbaren Schiffen, die er erfunden hatte und auf denen er segelte, erzählt hatte, und er begann zu denken, wie schrecklich es wäre, wenn alle es vergessen hätten und niemand wüsste, wofür die Party war;

and the more he thought like this, the more the party got muddled in his mind, like a dream when nothing goes right. 15.4

und je mehr er so dachte, desto mehr geriet die Party in seinem Kopf durcheinander, wie ein Traum, wenn nichts richtig läuft.

And the dream began to sing itself over in his head until it became a sort of song. 15.5

Und der Traum begann sich in seinem Kopf zu wiederholen, bis er zu einer Art Lied wurde.

It was an 15.6

Es war ein

ANXIOUS POOH SONG. 16.1

ÄNGSTLICHES PUUH-LIED.

3 Cheers for Pooh! 17.1

3 Prost auf Pooh!

18.1 **(For Who?)**
(Für wen?)

19.1 **For Pooh -**
Für Puh -

20.1 **(Why what did he do?)**
(Warum, was hat er getan?)

21.1 **I thought you knew;**
Ich dachte, Sie wüssten das;

22.1 **He saved his friend from a wetting!**
Er hat seinen Freund vor dem Einnässen bewahrt!

23.1 **3 Cheers for Bear!**
3 Prost auf Bär!

24.1 **(For where?)**
(Wozu?)

25.1 **For Bear -**
Für Bär -

26.1 **He couldn't swim,**
Er konnte nicht schwimmen,

27.1 **But he rescued him!**
Aber er hat ihn gerettet!

28.1 **(He rescued who?)**
(Wen hat er gerettet?)

Oh, listen, do!   29.1
Oh, hör zu, tu es!

I am talking of Pooh —   30.1
Ich spreche von Pooh —

(Of who?)   31.1
(Von wem?)

Of Pooh!   32.1
Von Pooh!

(I'm sorry I keep forgetting).   33.1
(Tut mir leid, dass ich das immer wieder vergesse).

Well, Pooh was a Bear of Enormous Brain   34.1
Nun, Pooh war ein Bär mit einem enormen Gehirn

(Just say it again!)   35.1
(Sagen Sie es einfach noch einmal!)

Of enormous brain -   36.1
Von enormer Gehirn -

(Of enormous what?)   37.1
(Von enormen was?)

Well, he ate a lot,   38.1
Nun, er hat viel gegessen,

39.1 **And I don't know if he could swim or not,**
Und ich weiß nicht, ob er schwimmen konnte oder nicht,

40.1 **But he managed to float**
Aber er schaffte es, zu schweben

41.1 **On a sort of boat**
Auf einer Art Boot

42.1 **(On a sort of what?)**
(Auf eine Art von was?)

43.1 **Well, a sort of pot —**
Nun, eine Art Topf —

44.1 **So now let's give him three hearty cheers**
Also lassen Sie uns dreimal herzlich auf ihn anstoßen

45.1 **(So now let's give him three hearty whiches?)**
(Und jetzt geben wir ihm drei herzhafte Brötchen?)

46.1 **And hope he'll be with us for years and years,**
Und ich hoffe, dass er uns noch viele Jahre erhalten bleibt,

47.1 **And grow in health and wisdom and riches!**
Und wachse an Gesundheit, Weisheit und Reichtum!

48.1 **3 Cheers for Pooh!**
3 Prost auf Pooh!

49.1 **(For who?)**
(Für wen?)

For Pooh -   50.1

Für Puh -

3 Cheers for Bear!   51.1

3 Prost auf Bär!

(For where?)   52.1

(Wozu?)

For Bear -   53.1

Für Bär -

3 Cheers for the wonderful Winnie-the-Pooh!   54.1

3 Prost auf den wunderbaren Winnie-the-Pooh!

(Just tell me, somebody - WHAT DID HE DO?)   55.1

(Sagt mir nur, dass jemand - WAS HAT ER GETAN?)

While this was going on inside him, Owl was talking   56.1
to Eeyore.

Während dies in ihm vor sich ging, sprach Eule mit I-Aah.

"Eeyore," said Owl, "Christopher Robin is giving a   57.1
party."

"I-Aah," sagte Eule, "Christopher Robin gibt eine Party."

"Very interesting," said Eeyore.   58.1

"Sehr interessant," sagte I-Aah.

"I suppose they will be sending me down the odd bits   58.2
which got trodden on.

"Ich nehme an, sie werden mir die Teile, die zertreten
wurden, hinunterschicken.

58.3 **Kind and Thoughtful. Not at all, don't mention it."**
Freundlich und nachdenklich. Keineswegs, keine
Ursache."

60.1 **"There is an Invitation for you."**
"Es gibt eine Einladung für Sie."

61.1 **"What's that like?"**
"Wie ist das so?"

62.1 **"An Invitation!"**
"Eine Einladung!"

"Yes, I heard you. Who dropped it?" 64.1

"Ja, ich habe Sie gehört. Wer hat es fallen lassen?"

"This isn't anything to eat, 65.1

"Das ist nichts zu essen,

it's asking you to the party. To- morrow." 65.2

sondern eine Einladung zu einer Party. Bis morgen."

Eeyore shook his head slowly. 66.1

Eeyore schüttelte langsam den Kopf.

"You mean Piglet. The little fellow with the excited 67.1
ears.

"Du meinst Ferkel. Der kleine Kerl mit den aufgeregten
Ohren.

That's Piglet. I'll tell him." 67.2

Das ist Ferkel. Ich werde es ihm sagen."

"No, no!" said Owl, getting quite fussy. 69.1

"Nein, nein!" sagte Eule und wurde ganz wählerisch.

69.2 "It's you!"
"Du bist es!"

70.1 "Are you sure?"
"Sind Sie sicher?"

71.1 "Of course I'm sure. Christopher Robin said,
"Natürlich bin ich mir sicher. Christopher Robin hat
gesagt,

71.2 'All of them! Tell all of them. "'
'Alle von ihnen! Sag es ihnen allen. "'

72.1 "All of them, except Eeyore?"
"Alle, außer I- Aah?"

73.1 "All of them," said Owl sulkily.
"Alle," sagte Eule mürrisch.

74.1 "Ah!" said Eeyore.
"Ah!" sagte I-Aah.

74.2 "A mistake, no doubt, but still, I shall come.
"Zweifellos ein Fehler, aber ich werde trotzdem kommen.

74.3 Only don't blame me if it rains."
Aber nimm es mir nicht übel, wenn es regnet."

75.1 But it didn't rain.
Aber es regnete nicht.

Christopher Robin had made a long table out of some long pieces of wood, 75.2

Christopher Robin hatte aus einigen langen Holzstücken einen langen Tisch gemacht,

and they all sat round it. 75.3

um den sie sich alle setzten.

Christopher Robin sat at one end, and Pooh sat at the other, and between them on one side were Owl and Eeyore and Piglet, and between them on the other side were Rabbit, and Roo and Kanga. 75.4

Christopher Robin saß an einem Ende und Puuh am anderen, und zwischen ihnen auf der einen Seite saßen Eule, I-Aah und Ferkel, und zwischen ihnen auf der anderen Seite Kaninchen, Ruh und Kanga.

And all Rabbit's friends and relations spread themselves about on the grass, and waited hopefully in case anybody spoke to them, or dropped anything, or asked them the time. 75.5

Und alle Freunde und Verwandten von Kaninchen verteilten sich auf dem Gras und warteten hoffnungsvoll, ob jemand sie ansprach, etwas fallen ließ oder nach der Uhrzeit fragte.

It was the first party to which Roo had ever been, and he was very excited. 76.1

Es war die erste Party, auf der Roo je gewesen war, und er war sehr aufgeregt.

As soon as ever they had sat down he began to talk. 76.2

Sobald sie sich hingesetzt hatten, begann er zu reden.

"Hallo, Pooh!" he squeaked. 77.1

"Hallo, Pooh!" quietschte er.

78.1 "Hallo, Roo!" said Pooh.
"Hallo, Ruh!" sagte Puuh.

79.1 Roo jumped up and down in his seat for a little while
and then began again.
Roo hüpfte eine Weile in seinem Sitz auf und ab und begann
dann wieder.

80.1 "Hallo, Piglet!" he squeaked.
"Hallo, Ferkel!" quietschte er.

81.1 Piglet waved a paw at him, being too busy to say
anything.
Ferkel winkte ihm mit einer Pfote zu, da es zu beschäftigt
war, um etwas zu sagen.

82.1 "Hallo, Eeyore!" said Roo.
"Hallo, I-Aah!" sagte Ruh.

83.1 Eeyore nodded gloomily at him.
Eeyore nickte ihm düster zu.

83.2 "It will rain soon, you see if it doesn't, "
"Es wird bald regnen, du wirst sehen, wenn es nicht
regnet, "

83.3 he said.
sagte er.

84.1 Roo looked to see if it didn't, and it didn't, so he said
Ruh schaute nach, um zu sehen, ob es nicht so war, und es
war nicht so, also sagte er

"Hallo, Owl!" - and Owl said   84.2

"Hallo, Eule!" - und Eule sagte freundlich

"Hallo, my little fellow,"   84.3

"Hallo, mein kleiner Freund"

in a kindly way, and went on telling Christopher   84.4
Robin about an accident which had nearly happened
to a friend of his whom Christopher Robin didn't
know, and Kanga said to Roo,

und fuhr fort, Christopher Robin von einem Unfall zu
erzählen, der einem seiner Freunde, den Christopher
Robin nicht kannte, beinahe passiert wäre, und Kanga
sagte zu Ruh,

"Drink up your milk first, dear, and talk afterwards." 84.5

"Trink erst deine Milch aus, Schatz, und rede danach."

So Roo, who was drinking his milk, tried to say that   84.6
he could do both at once ...

Daraufhin versuchte Ruh, der gerade seine Milch trank, zu
sagen, dass er beides auf einmal tun könne ...

and had to be patted on the back and dried for quite a 84.7
long time afterwards.

und musste danach ziemlich lange auf den Rücken geklopft
und abgetrocknet werden.

298

86.1 When they had all nearly eaten enough, Christopher
Robin banged on the table with his spoon, and
everybody stopped talking and was very silent,
except Roo who was just finishing a loud attack of
hiccups and trying to look as if it was one of Rabbit's
relations.

Als sie alle fast genug gegessen hatten, schlug Christopher
Robin mit seinem Löffel auf den Tisch, und alle hörten auf
zu reden und waren ganz still, außer Ruh, der gerade einen
lauten Schluckaufanfall hatte und versuchte, so zu tun, als
sei er ein Verwandter von Rabbit.

88.1 "This party," said Christopher Robin,

"Diese Party," sagte Christopher Robin,

88.2 "is a party because of what someone did, and we all
know who it was, and it's his party, because of what
he did, and I've got a present for him and here it is."

"ist eine Party wegen etwas, das jemand getan hat, und wir
alle wissen, wer es war, und es ist seine Party, wegen dem,
was er getan hat, und ich habe ein Geschenk für ihn, und
hier ist es."

Then he felt about a little and whispered, "Where is it?"

88.3

Dann tastete er ein wenig herum und flüsterte, "Wo ist es?"

While he was looking,

89.1

Während er sich umsah,

Eeyore coughed in an impressive way and began to speak.

89.2

hustete Eeyore auf beeindruckende Weise und begann zu sprechen.

"Friends," he said,

90.1

"Freunde," sagte er,

"including oddments, it is a great pleasure, or perhaps I had better say it has been a pleasure so far, to see you at my party.

90.2

"es ist eine große Freude, oder vielleicht sollte ich besser sagen, es war bisher eine Freude, Sie auf meiner Party zu sehen.

What I did was nothing. Any of you -

90.3

Was ich getan habe, war gar nichts. Jeder von euch -

except Rabbit and Owl and Kanga - would have done the same. Oh,

90.4

außer Kaninchen, Eule und Kanga - hätte dasselbe getan. Oh,

and Pooh.

90.5

und Puuh.

My remarks do not, of course, apply to Piglet and Roo, because they are too small.

90.6

Meine Bemerkungen gelten natürlich nicht für Ferkel und Ruh, weil sie zu klein sind.

90.7 Any of you would have done the same.
Jeder von euch hätte das Gleiche getan.

90.8 But it just happened to be Me.
Aber es war nun einmal ich.

90.9 It was not, I need hardly say, with an idea of getting
what Christopher Robin is looking for now" — and
he put his front leg to his mouth and said in a loud
whisper, "Try under the table" — "that I did what I
did — but because I feel that we should all do what we
can to help.
Ich brauche wohl kaum zu sagen, dass ich das nicht getan
habe, um das zu bekommen, wonach Christopher Robin
jetzt sucht" - und er legte sein Vorderbein an seinen Mund
und sagte laut flüsternd, "Versuch es unter dem Tisch" -
"sondern weil ich finde, dass wir alle tun sollten, was wir
können, um zu helfen.

90.10 I feel that we should all —— "
Ich finde, wir sollten alle …"

91.1 "H — hup!" said Roo accidentally.
"H — hup!" sagte Roo versehentlich.

92.1 "Roo, dear!" said Kanga reproachfully.
"Ruh, mein Lieber!" sagte Kanga vorwurfsvoll.

93.1 "Was it me?" asked Roo, a little surprised.
"War ich das?" fragte Roo ein wenig überrascht.

94.1 "What's Eeyore talking about?" Piglet whispered to
Pooh.
"Wovon redet I-Aah?" flüsterte Ferkel Puuh zu.

"I don't know," said Pooh rather dolefully. 95.1

"Ich weiß nicht," sagte Pooh etwas bedrückt.

"I thought this was your party." 96.1

"Ich dachte, das wäre deine Party."

"I thought it was once. 97.1

"Ich dachte, das war einmal.

But I suppose it isn't." 97.2

Aber ich nehme an, das ist es nicht."

"I'd sooner it was yours than Eeyore's," said Piglet. 98.1

"Lieber du als I-Aah," sagte Ferkel.

"So would I," said Pooh. 99.1

"Das würde ich auch," sagte Pooh.

"H — hup!" said Roo again. 100.1

"H — hup!" sagte Roo wieder.

"AS — I — WAS — SAYING," said Eeyore loudly and 101.1
sternly,

"Wie ich schon sagte," sagte I-Aah laut und streng,

"as I was saying when I was interrupted by various 101.2
Loud Sounds, I feel that —— "

"als ich durch verschiedene laute Geräusche unterbrochen
wurde, habe ich das Gefühl, dass ..."

"Here it is!" cried Christopher Robin excitedly. 102.1

"Hier ist es!" rief Christopher Robin aufgeregt.

302

102.2 "Pass it down to silly old Pooh. It's for Pooh."
"Gib es dem dummen, alten Pooh weiter. Es ist für Pooh."

103.1 "For Pooh?" said Eeyore.
"Für Puuh?" sagte I-Aah.

104.1 "Of course it is. The best bear in all the world."
"Natürlich ist er das. Der beste Bär auf der ganzen Welt."

105.1 "I might have known," said Eeyore.
"Das hätte ich mir denken können," sagte I-Aah.

105.2 "After all, one can't complain.
"Schließlich kann man sich nicht beklagen.

105.3 I have my friends.
Ich habe meine Freunde.

105.4 Somebody spoke to me only yesterday.
Jemand hat erst gestern mit mir gesprochen.

105.5 And was it last week or the week before that Rabbit bumped into me and said,
Und war es letzte Woche oder vorletzte Woche, als der Hase mich anrempelte und sagte,

105.6 'Bother!' The Social Round. Always something going on."
'Mist!' Die soziale Runde. Da ist immer was los."

Nobody was listening, for they were all saying "Open it, Pooh," 107.1

Niemand hörte zu, denn alle sagten, "Mach's auf, Puuh,"

"What is it, Pooh?" 107.2

"Was ist das, Puuh?"

"I know what it is," 107.3

"Ich weiß, was es ist,"

"No, you don't" 107.4

"Nein, das weißt du nicht"

and other helpful remarks of this sort. 107.5

und andere hilfreiche Bemerkungen dieser Art.

And of course Pooh was opening it as quickly as ever he could, but without cutting the string, because you never know when a bit of string might be Useful. 107.6

Und natürlich öffnete Puuh es so schnell er konnte, ohne die Schnur zu zerschneiden, denn man weiß ja nie, wann ein Stückchen Schnur nützlich sein könnte.

At last it was undone. 107.7

Endlich war er offen.

108.1 When Pooh saw what it was, he nearly fell down, he
was so pleased.
Als Puuh sah, was es war, fiel er vor lauter Freude fast um.

108.2 It was a Special Pencil Case.
Es war ein besonderes Federmäppchen.

108.3 There were pencils in it marked "B" for Bear,
Darin befanden sich Bleistifte mit der Aufschrift "B" für
Bär,

108.4 and pencils marked "HB"
Bleistifte mit der Aufschrift "HB"

108.5 for Helping Bear, and pencils marked "BB"
für Helfender Bär und Bleistifte mit der Aufschrift "BB"

108.6 for Brave Bear.
für Tapferer Bär.

108.7 There was a knife for sharpening the pencils, and
india-rubber for rubbing out anything which you had
spelt wrong, and a ruler for ruling lines for the words
to walk on, and inches marked on the ruler in case
you wanted to know how many inches anything was,
and Blue Pencils and Red Pencils and Green Pencils
for saying special things in blue and red and green.
Es gab ein Messer, um die Stifte anzuspitzen, und ein
Radiergummi, um alles auszuradieren, was man falsch
geschrieben hatte, und ein Lineal, um Linien für die
Wörter zu ziehen, auf denen man laufen konnte, und
Zollmarkierungen auf dem Lineal, falls man wissen wollte,
wie viele Zoll etwas war, und blaue Bleistifte und rote
Bleistifte und grüne Bleistifte, um besondere Dinge in blau
und rot und grün zu schreiben.

And all these lovely things were in little pockets of
their own in a Special Case which shut with a click
when you clicked it.

108.8

Und all diese schönen Dinge befanden sich in eigenen
kleinen Taschen in einem besonderen Etui, das sich mit
einem Klicken schloss, wenn man es anklickte.

And they were all for Pooh.

108.9

Und sie waren alle für Puuh.

"Oh!" said Pooh.

109.1

"Oh!" sagte Puuh.

"Oh, Pooh!" said everybody else except Eeyore.

110.1

"Oh, Puuh!" sagten alle außer I-Aah.

"Thank-you," growled Pooh.

111.1

"Danke," knurrte Pooh.

But Eeyore was saying to himself, "This writing
business.

112.1

Aber I-Aah sagte zu sich selbst, "Dieses Schreibgeschäft.

Pencils and what-not. Over-rated, if you ask me.

112.2

Bleistifte und so weiter. Überbewertet, wenn du mich
fragst.

Silly stuff. Nothing in it."

112.3

Albernes Zeug. Da ist nichts drin."

113.1 Later on, when they had all said "Good-bye" and
"Thank-you" to Christopher Robin, Pooh and Piglet
walked home thoughtfully together in the golden
evening, and for a long time they were silent.

Später, als sich alle von Christopher Robin verabschiedet
und bedankt hatten, gingen Puuh und Ferkel im goldenen
Abendlicht nachdenklich nach Hause und schwiegen lange
Zeit.

115.1 "When you wake up in the morning, Pooh," said
Piglet at last,

"Wenn du morgens aufwachst, Puuh," sagte Ferkel
schließlich,

115.2 "what's the first thing you say to yourself?"

"was ist das Erste, was du zu dir sagst?"

116.1 "What's for breakfast?" said Pooh.

"Was gibt es zum Frühstück?" fragte Puuh.

116.2 "What do you say, Piglet?"

"Was sagst du dazu, Ferkel?"

"I say, I wonder what's going to happen exciting to-day?"

"Ich frage mich, was heute wohl Spannendes passieren wird?"

117.1

said Piglet.

sagte Ferkel.

117.2

Pooh nodded thoughtfully.

Puuh nickte nachdenklich.

118.1

"It's the same thing," he said.

"Das ist dasselbe," sagte er.

119.1

"And what did happen?" asked Christopher Robin.

"Und was ist passiert?" fragte Christopher Robin.

121.1

"When?"

"Wann?"

122.1

"Next morning."

"Am nächsten Morgen."

123.1

"I don't know."

"Ich weiß es nicht."

124.1

"Could you think and tell me and Pooh some time?"

"Könntest du nachdenken und es mir und Pooh irgendwann sagen?"

125.1

126.1 **"If you wanted it very much."**
"Wenn Sie es unbedingt wollten."

127.1 **"Pooh does," said Christopher Robin.**
"Pooh schon," sagte Christopher Robin.

128.1 **He gave a deep sigh, picked his bear up by the leg
and walked off to the door, trailing Winnie-the-Pooh
behind him.**
Er seufzte tief, nahm seinen Bären an den Beinen und ging
zur Tür, Winnie-the-Pooh hinter sich herziehend.

128.2 **At the door he turned and said,**
An der Tür drehte er sich um und sagte,

128.3 **"Coming to see me have my bath?"**
"Willst du sehen, wie ich gebadet werde?"

129.1 **"I might," I said.**
"Vielleicht," sagte ich.

130.1 **"Was Pooh's pencil case any better than mine?"**
"War Poohs Federmäppchen besser als meins?"

131.1 **"It was just the same," I said.**
"Es war genau dasselbe," sagte ich.
·

132.1 **He nodded and went out ...**
Er nickte und ging hinaus ...

132.2 **and in a moment I heard Winnie-the- Pooh -**
und einen Moment später hörte ich Winnie-the- Pooh -

bump, bump, bump - going up the stairs behind him.   132.3

bump, bump, bump - hinter ihm die Treppe hinaufgehen.

Möwenstein Books

www.mowenstein.com

Renowned Authors

H. G. Wells · Ernest Hemingway
H. P. Lovecraft · Lewis Carroll
Franz Kafka · Friedrich Nietzsche
Albert Einstein · Oscar Wilde
Hans Christian Andersen

Notable Works

Frankenstein · *Alice in Wonderland*
Heart of Darkness · *The Great Gatsby*
Siddhartha · *The Metamorphosis*
Thus Spoke Zarathustra

Translation Services

We offer translation services in various languages, including German, Spanish, Chinese, Korean, Arabic, and more. For custom translations or revisions, please contact us at:

Email: translation@mowenstein.com

Our Collections

Franz Kafka Collection

- *The Metamorphosis / Die Verwandlung*
- *The Trial / Der Prozess*
- *The Castle / Das Schloss*
- *and many more...*

Pakt mit dem Teufel

- *Faust Parts I & II* by Johann Wolfgang von Goethe
- *Doctor Faustus* by Christopher Marlowe

Portraits of Irishmen

- *The Picture of Dorian Gray* by Oscar Wilde
- *A Portrait of the Artist as a Young Man* by James Joyce

Children's Classics

- *Winnie-the-Pooh / Pu der Bär*
- *Brothers Grimm Fairy Tales*
- *Fairy Tales Told for Children*
  - Author: Hans Christian Andersen

Visit Us

At Möwenstein Books, we are committed to providing high-quality bilingual editions of classic works. Explore our collections and discover more titles across various genres and languages.

Website: www.mowenstein.com